DWARFS

A WARHAMMER ARMIES SUPPLEMENT

DWARFS

CONTENTS

A MAP OF THE DWARF REALMS 4

THE DWARF THRONG 6
    Dwarf Warriors 6
    Slayers 7
    Runesmiths & the Anvil of Doom 8
    Thunderers & Rangers 10
    Miners. 11
    Hammerers 12
    Iron Breakers & Long Beards 13
    The Engineers Guild 14
    Flame Cannon. 15
    Dwarf Organ Gun 16
    Gyrocopter 17
DWARF ARMOURY 18
DWARF RUNES 18
    Runic Magic 18
    Creating a Rune Item 19
    Weapon Runes 20
    Armour Runes. 21
    Runic Banners. 21
    Engineering Runes 22
    Runic Talismans 23

FORCES OF THE DWARFS 24
    Lords. 26
    Heroes 27
    Core Units. 28
    Special Units 30
    Rare Units 32
PAINTING THE DWARF ARMY 33
DWARFS OF LEGEND 49
    Thorek Ironbrow, Dwarf Runelord 50
    King Alrik Ranulfsson 52
THE DWARF REALMS 55
    The Gates of Karaz-A-Karak. 56
    Barak Varr 59
    Travels through the Worlds Edge Mountains. 60
    Karak Azgal. 64
    Dwarfs at War. 66
    Dwarfs Abroad 69
    The War of the Beard 70
    The Dwarf Tongue 72
    Leading Your Dwarfs 76
    Armies of the Dwarfs 78
    Reference page. 80

Written by
Gav Thorpe
& Alessio Cavatore

With
Rick Priestley, Tuomas Pirinen,
Space McQuirk & Jake Thornton

Cover Illustration
Paul Dainton

Illustrators
John Blanche,
Alex Boyd, Paul Dainton,
Karl Kopinski & Adrian Smith

Graphics
Nuala Kennedy

Citadel Designers
Tim Adcock, Colin Dixon,
Aly Morrison & Michael Perry

Model Makers
Dave Andrews & Mark Jones

Miniatures Painters
Owen Branham, Neil Green,
Martin Footitt, Keith Robertson,
Chris Smart, Kirsten Mickelburgh
Dave Thomas & Tammy Haye

Invaluable Grudgeness
Alan Merrett

PRODUCED BY GAMES WORKSHOP

Alrik Ranulfsson, Anvil of Doom, Burlok Damminson, Citadel & the Citadel castle, 'Eavy Metal, Games Workshop & the Games Workshop logo, Gotrek Gurnisson, Felix Jaeger, Hammerer, Iron Breaker, Josef Bugman, Long Beard, the Old World, Runelord, Skaven, Thorek Ironbrow, Thorgrim Grudgebearer, Throne of Power, Thunderer, Troll Slayer Ungrim Ironfist and Warhammer are trademarks of Games Workshop Ltd.
'Scatter' dice are UK registered design no. 2017484.
All artwork in all Games Workshop products and the images contained therein have been produced either in-house or as work for hire. The copyright in the artwork and the images it depicts is the exclusive property of Games Workshop Ltd.
All rights reserved. No part of this publication may be reproduced, stored in a retrieval system, or transmitted in any form or by any means, electronic, mechanical, photocopying, recording or otherwise, without the prior permission of Games Workshop. Copyright Games Workshop Ltd., 2000.
British cataloguing-in-Publication Data. A catalogue record for this book is available from the British Library.

UK	US	Australia	Canada
Games Workshop,	Games Workshop,	Games Workshop,	1645 Bonhill Rd,
Willow Rd,	6721 Baymeadow Drive,	23 Liverpool Street,	Units 9-11,
Lenton,	Glen Burnie,	Ingleburn	Mississauga,
Nottingham, NG7 2WS	Maryland, 21060-6401	NSW 2565	Ontario, L5T 1R3

Games Workshop World Wide Web site: www.games-workshop.com   ISBN: 1-84154-066-8

INTRODUCTION

The Dwarfs have been waging war for over 4,000 years. Theirs is a sorrowful tale of a once great empire which has slowly been worn down by the constant struggle against Goblins, Skaven and other foul races. Over the course of many centuries they have fought with a grim determination to defend their realm. It is a bitter struggle against a foe whose numbers never seem to dwindle, and many of their magnificent Holds have fallen into the hands of their enemies. Still they fight on, for such is the courage and resolve of these brave warriors that one day they truly believe that their empire will be great again.

This book deals with the armies of the Dwarfs and offers you all the information that you will need to lead a force of these courageous warriors into battle. The Dwarf army is an easy force to use but a difficult one to master; you will need to be an experienced general to learn the tactics required to deal with the many foes that will assault your battle lines. The Dwarfs are a stout race whose tough resolve makes them a difficult force to conquer. Their lack of speed is more than compensated by their stoic determination. Masters in the art of forging metals, they build great machines of destruction to rain death upon their foe before they reach the Dwarfs' line of defence, and if the enemy finally does assault the Dwarf formations, they will crash against a solid wall of armour.

As a Dwarf general you do not have the luxury of fast cavalry with which to outflank an opponent. Neither do you have any monstrous beasts which can strike terror into the hearts of the enemy. You must make the best use of your disciplined infantry to anticipate your opponent's every move, defending against his attacks and counter-attacking when he is at his weakest. You will find the Dwarfs an army that you can depend on. The rewards of collecting a Dwarf army are immense and more than worthwhile.

Inside this book you will find the following sections:

THE DWARF THRONG
Here can be found descriptions and rules for all of the many warriors and engines of destruction that can be found in a Dwarf army.

DWARF ARMOURY
Rules for new weapons and armour of the Dwarfs.

DWARF RUNES (MAGIC ITEMS)
Full rules for creating powerful runic magic items.

FORCES OF THE DWARFS (ARMY LIST)
How to field a Dwarf army in Warhammer.

PAINTING THE DWARF ARMY
Photographs of the splendid Citadel Miniatures Dwarfs, with advice on assembling and painting your own Dwarf Throng.

THE DWARF REALMS
An in-depth look at the lands of the Dwarf empire, its traditions, history and peoples.

THE DWARF THRONG

DWARF WARRIORS

Durgrim Redmane cast an eye over the crowd, ignoring the snores of the weak-headed who had already succumbed to the ale.

"Course," he declared to those still conscious, "the real test of a Dwarf's mettle is in battle. Like as not some of you young 'uns have been called up by the Thanes to fight, like all Dwarfs are sworn to do. Aye, that's a sight and a half – seeing the ranks of the Hold arrayed for war, their fine armour and well-forged weapons gleaming in the lamplight."

He sighed deeply at the thought before taking another tremendous gulp of beer from the horn in his calloused hand.

"Still, back in the old days, there were armies the likes of which you've never seen, and even the shortbeards like you soft 'uns were hardened warriors. Utterly loyal, they was, not come and go as you please like some folk I could mention. Sturdy fighters, respectful of their Thanes and King, sworn to lay down their lives in the defence of the Hold, staunch in the face of the greatest dangers. Stand fast against anything they would; nary a dragon or a great daemon would cause them to raise an eyebrow, and perish the cur who thought of saving his own life before protecting his kinsmen."

> ## DWARF SPECIAL RULES
>
> The following special rules apply to **all** the models in a Dwarf army.
>
> **Ancestral Grudge.** Dwarfs hold grudges for a long time, possibly forever. They have never forgiven the fall of their strongholds at the hands of the Orcish enemy. Dwarfs *hate* all types of Orcs, Goblins and Snotlings, including Night Goblins, Black Orcs, Hobgoblins... in fact all greenskins of any description!
>
> **Resolute.** Dwarfs fight with grim determination and are slow to abandon their position. Dwarfs flee and pursue 2D6-1" instead of the normal 2D6".
>
> **Relentless.** A Dwarf on the march is as implacable as the turning of the years, and just as impossible to halt. Dwarf units may march even if there are enemy within 8".

Redmane downed the remainder of his ale and wiped the froth from his beard on his sleeve.

"Like a well-crafted mail shirt a Dwarf army is, each warrior an iron-hard link, knitted together by duty, respect and loyalty. And, like a mail shirt, never a blow shall pass them as long as all the links remain strong."

He looked accusingly at the assembled youngsters.

"No weak links here, I hope..."

There was a cry of disapproval and proclamations of courage rang from the low rafters of the tavern and set the shields on the wall to shaking.

"That's what I thought."

Dwarfs live in family units called **clans**. In times of war these clans muster together any Dwarf old enough to fight and form into regiments. The warriors of these regiments are expected to maintain their own armour and weapons, which are often ancient family heirlooms which have been handed down through the generations and presented to the Dwarf when he comes of age.

DWARF WARRIORS

	M	WS	BS	S	T	W	I	A	Ld
Dwarf Lord	3	7	4	4	5	3	4	4	10
Dwarf Thane	3	6	4	4	4	2	3	3	9
Dwarf Veteran	3	4	3	3	4	1	2	2	9
Dwarf Warrior	3	4	3	3	4	1	2	1	9
Crossbowman	3	4	3	3	4	1	2	1	9

THE DWARF THRONG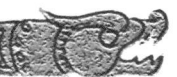

SLAYERS

Leaning back in his chair the old Dwarf cleared his throat with a deep cough.

"Back before you were mere lusty twinkles in your father's eye, I was fighting Goblins at the shores of the Black Water pool. A warrior at the young age of one hundred, I was proud to be fighting with the High King and his kin. Those were the days, when Goblins were real Goblins, not like the skinny green wretches you get nowadays."

Redmane pulled a pipe from his pocket handing it to one of his audience to fill.

"Now as I was saying, before the High King was treacherously pulled to his sad demise over the icy falls, I was lucky enough to meet a Slayer bearing the name of Garaith Ungrim. It was from him that I learned of the tale of the very first Slayer; Gudrun was his name, and he was best friend to King Skorri Morgrimson. The pair had grown up together as beardlings and fought side by side in many a battle. That having been said, you can imagine the honour that he felt when the King asked him to protect his only son Furgil as he attempted to infiltrate the lower halls of Karak Ungor. Swearing an oath to his King, Gudrun followed Furgil on his mission. When the party was ambushed by a band of Night Goblins accompanied by a huge Troll, Gudrun fought valiantly to save his Prince's life. It is said that over sixty of the vile Grobi lay at his feet but still they came until a lucky blow struck Gudrun unconscious. As blackness enveloped his eyes, he saw Furgil being carried away by the Troll."

The small crowd that had gathered around Durgrim sat in silence enraptured by his tale.

"When he awoke he found himself alone, the Goblins had left him for dead although they had stolen his hammer and even robbed the very boots from his feet. Gudrun tracked the Troll, treading barefoot down through the dark depths of Karak Ungor until he found its lair. Upon discovering the slain mutilated body of the Dwarf prince, such was Gudrun's rage that he took the dead prince's rune-axe and beheaded the vile Troll with a single blow. Gudrun's shame upon failing to protect his ward was so deep that he knew he could never return to Karaz-a-Karak and face the King. Now before his murder, Prince Furgil sported a deep fiery red beard that was the envy of every Dwarf this side of the Worlds Edge Mountains. In his grief Gudrun dyed his own hair orange in respect to the fallen prince. Unable to fulfil his oath to his King, Gudrun wandered the mountains. Seeking death as a release from his sorrow, he spent the remainder of his years hunting down and slaying every Troll that he could find. To this day, Dwarfs unable to fulfil an oath still dye their hair bright orange and wield an axe in respect of Gudrun and Furgil. As for Gudrun, no one knows of his fate, but none shall forget his name."

Old Redmane sucked on the large pipe which had been filled and lit for him. "Call this pipeweed!" *He coughed out a great billow of musky smelling smoke.* "I've smoked hay that tasted better."

Dwarfs are very proud individuals and do not cope well with failure or personal loss. When a tragedy occurs, a Dwarf may be driven to take the oath of the Slayer. He will break all ties with his Hold and his clan and seek death by hunting down and fighting a monstrous beast. Many achieve their wish to die at the hands of a foul creature, but some survive to fight more beasts until the day they meet their final destiny.

SLAYERS

	M	WS	BS	S	T	W	I	A	Ld
Daemon Slayer	3	7	3	4	5	3	5	4	10
Dragon Slayer	3	6	3	4	4	2	4	3	10
Giant Slayer	3	5	3	4	4	1	3	2	10
Troll Slayer	3	4	3	3	4	1	2	1	10

Slayer Champions. Any Slayer regiment may have as many Giant Slayers as you wish – the normal limitation of having only one Champion per regiment does not apply to Slayers.

Special Rules

Unbreakable. See the Warhammer rulebook, p112. Note however that Slayers still *hate* greenskins.

Loner. Daemon Slayers and Dragon Slayers may only fight alone or join a Slayers unit. Daemon and Dragon Slayers can never be the army's General.

Slayer. All Slayers have an uncanny ability which makes them particularly effective against especially tough opponents. When rolling to wound, a Slayer's Strength, including any modifiers for weapons (eg, a Great Axe), is increased until it is equal to the Toughness of his opponent, up to a maximum of Strength 6. If the opponent's Toughness is lower than the Slayer's Strength, including any modifiers for weapons, the Slayer does not receive any Strength bonus. For example, a Slayer armed with a Great Axe (S5) is fighting a Dragon (T6): normally he needs a 5+ to wound, but because of the Slayer skill his Strength is increased to 6 and he therefore wounds on a 4+. Note that the armour save modifier is calculated at the modified Strength score, in this case it is -3 for a Strength 6 hit. If the Slayer were fighting a weedy Goblin (T3), he would use his normal Strength of 5 and would therefore wound the Goblin on a 2+, with an armour save modifier of -2.

7

RUNESMITHS

"Well, if you ask me, it's all that dabbling with wizards and their like that has all them other races in such a poor state," Redmane continued, lugging a keg of ale from the bar and thudding it down on the table in front of him.

"No true Dwarf has truck with that kind of wild magic, oh no. In the olden days our ancestors realised the perils of dabbling with the forces of magic in its raw form, and they knew best. Runes they made, powerful runes to capture the magic, not let it float about all willy-nilly where it could do no end of harm. Everything had runes on in them days, not like now where they're something rare and special. Even had me a rune-lamp once, and a rune-cloak, but now there isn't the Runesmith who can make 'em."

The old Hammerer prised the top off the beer keg and dipped his drinking horn into the foamy, lumpy liquid within.

"The Runesmiths you see, they's a rare breed now, and getting rarer. And the magic, that's going too. Only the Runelords, the venerable ones with a good five hundred years under their belt, only they can try to make really powerful runes these days. Was a time when an apprentice would be forging them types of runes, but not nowadays. I remember great-great-great-uncle Snaddri had a rune-axe that could take the top off a mountain if he had a mind to do it, which he didn't 'cause attacking mountains is something only a daft Manling would do. Still, them Runelords have got their Anvils of Doom, keep them in good shape still. Lug one of them up to the battle and you'll see what good old fashioned rune lore was like, not like the cantrips and petty nonsense you'll get today."

Runesmiths are ancient and powerful individuals and as such are accorded a great status within their stronghold. It takes hundreds of years for an apprentice to master the skills necessary to forge a rune. They uphold family traditions of working metal and magic into mighty runes of power.

RUNESMITHS

	M	WS	BS	S	T	W	I	A	Ld
Runelord	3	6	4	4	5	3	3	2	10
Runesmith	3	5	4	4	4	2	2	2	9

Special Rules
Rune Lore. A Runesmith or Runelord gives the Dwarf player an extra Dispel dice in the enemy Magic phase.

ANVIL OF DOOM

The Anvils of Doom are ancient devices forged with great skill by the Runesmiths of old in the bowels of Thunder Mountain. Using the energy of the volcano's heart, Kurgaz, the most skilled of the old ones, melted gromril to forge the anvils. As they cooled, Kurgaz beat the Rune of Sorcery onto each gleaming anvil.

No one knows how many anvils were forged before the secret of the Rune of Sorcery was lost. The Dwarf Book of Grudges records how an evil dragon attacked Thunder Mountain and slew the old Runesmith in a mighty battle which rent the mountain apart. During the devastation, the forges of Thunder Mountain were destroyed and many Runesmiths slain. In present times, the Anvils of Doom are ancient and valuable heirlooms, and the Dwarfs value them more highly than any of their other possessions.

Runesmiths use the Anvils of Doom for making magic items. Most anvils are owned by the various strongholds or by the Guilds, and the Runesmiths make use of these when they need to. A few Anvils are owned by Runesmiths, but these tend to be the sedentary Runesmiths who reside in the halls of Karaz-a-Karak and the weapon shops of Karak Azul.

The Anvils are objects of great power, and in times of extreme need a Runesmith can unleash fire and lightning upon his foes. With a mighty blow of his hammer, the Runesmith can release the Anvil's power.

ANVIL OF DOOM

	M	WS	BS	S	T	W	I	A	Ld
Anvil Guard	3	5	3	4	4	1	2	2	10

THE ANVIL IN THE GAME

A Dwarf army may have one and **only** one Anvil of Doom. In gaming terms, the Anvil is treated as a piece of terrain; it cannot be moved or attacked at all (no more than you can move or attack a hill!).

The Runelord and the two Anvil Guards would rather give their lives before abandoning this most ancient artefact, and must remain for all the battle on the platform. They are Unbreakable, may not declare charges and will never pursue beaten foes. The Anvil and crew have a Unit Strength of 3.

Enemy units which charge the Anvil model are placed in base contact with the platform. The Runelord and the Guards place themselves between the enemy and the anvil, without leaving the Anvil's platform. The Anvil and crew count as a unit with a 60mm wide frontage for the purposes of who can fight who (this is the width of the Anvil's base).

When shooting at the Anvil of Doom, randomise hits evenly between the remaining Dwarfs. To take into account the protection offered by the Anvil, the Runelord gains a 4+ Ward save against any form of missile (this includes magic missiles as well as normal missiles).

If the Runelord and Guards are killed, the enemy scores the points of the Anvil (plus an extra 100 Victory points if they are killed in close combat). If the Runelord is killed but there is still at least one Guard alive at the end of the game, the enemy scores the points for the Runelord, but not the points for the Anvil.

THE ANVIL AND THE DWARF MAGIC PHASE

During his own Magic phase the Dwarf player receives D6+2 Power dice. During the enemy's Magic phase everything is as normal, though the Anvil adds an extra dice to the Dwarfs' Dispel pool.

The Runelord uses the powers of the Anvil of Doom by striking the appropriate elemental rune upon it. In gaming terms, the Runelord may cast each of the four runic powers one per Magic phase using the Power dice provided by the Anvil. He may use a maximum of four dice to power a runic spell. If the Runelord is fighting in close combat, he will not be able to cast runic spells. If the spell is miscast, the Runelord does not have to roll on the Miscast table, but the Dwarf Magic phase ends immediately and all remaining dice are discarded.

RUNIC POWERS   Casting Value

Rune of Water   6+
When struck properly, the Anvil's magic pulses out into the ground, drawing water from underground lakes and rivers and causing it to swell up onto the battlefield to create a mire. This power can be cast on any enemy unit on the tabletop. The unit's Movement is halved until the end of its own following turn. If forced to flee, for whatever reason, the unit flees at half speed (determine the flee distance of the unit as normal and then halve the score, rounding up). This spell has no effect on flyers or ethereal creatures.

Rune of Air   7+
If successfully struck, this rune causes a dark cloud to gather over the battlefield and a storm of lightning cascades down upon an enemy unit. This spell can be cast on any enemy unit on the tabletop, causing D6 Strength 4 hits. These hits are distributed exactly like hits from shooting.

Rune of Fire   8+
Each blow of the Runelord's hammer causes a fiery ball to explode into his foes. This rune releases a *magic missile* with a range of 30". If successfully cast, the fireball causes 2D6 Strength 4 hits.

Rune of Earth   9+
The clang of hammer on rune reverberates across the battlefield, causing the ground to tremble before exploding under the enemy in a hail of rocky shards. This spell can be cast on any enemy unit within line of sight. The Anvil causes D6 Strength 5 hits on any one enemy unit on the tabletop, plus a further D6 Strength 5 hits if the unit is partially or wholly within a rocky feature (all hills, rocky outcrops, ruins, or any similar area which has been identified as high ground, rocky or ruinous before the game).

Lightning strikes as mighty energies unfurl, the sky darkens with brooding energy and clouds of multi-coloured magic swirl and sparkle in the air.

A Runelord, one of the oldest and most revered Runesmiths, may bring an Anvil to battle. The Anvil is mounted on its own platform, normally deployed on a dominating hill overseeing the battlefield, and the Runelord stands proudly beside it. The Anvil is protected by two Dwarf Anvil Guards who have sworn to defend it to the death.

The Dwarf army can use the Anvil to draw energy from the winds of magic, the nebulous source of magic power that flows over the battlefield. Just as Wizards draw upon the winds of magic to cast their spells, the Anvil absorbs magical energy to power the runes engraved upon it.

THUNDERERS

"Now, don't get me wrong, I'd rather be on the right end of a handgun than the wrong end, but what's wrong with proper, old-fashioned crossbows?"

The old Hammerer was mumbling to himself as much as talking to the Dwarfs around him.

"I mean, it makes an awful stink, for Grungni's sake, and smoke everywhere, stings your eyes something rotten it does. Still, they're better than those contraptions the Manlings cart about these days – least you can hit something at fifty paces. Crossbows have been around for thousands of years, but you youngsters have your heads turned by the latest whiz-bang to come out of the Engineers guild. Progress, they calls it. Fixing what isn't broken, I've half a mind to say."

Some clans are rich enough to purchase handguns from the Engineers Guild. Extremely proud of these weapons, they go to great lengths to maintain them. Dwarf handguns are exceptional works of craftsmanship and are more accurate than the shoddy constructions of the Empire.

THUNDERERS

	M	WS	BS	S	T	W	I	A	Ld
Thunderer	3	4	3	3	4	1	2	1	9
Veteran	3	4	3	3	4	1	2	2	9

RANGERS

"That's a well made crossbow," exclaimed Redmane, turning the weapon over in his hands and examining it carefully. "Hunting design, if I'm not mistaken. You practising to be a Ranger, lad?" he asked the owner, who nodded slightly, unsure whether this would meet with the old Dwarf's approval or not.

"Something odd about a Dwarf who likes being up on the surface all day, hunting and such. In the olden days we wouldn't have gone above ground for more than an hour unless we had to. All that sun and air's bad for your health you know, and there's plenty a Ranger gone missing never to return. Course, some say they got sun-touched and wandered off, others think the Trolls and Orcs got them. Who am I to say?"

The would-be Ranger shrugged and made a half-hearted attempt to retrieve his crossbow but it was drawn just out of reach as Redmane turned towards the bar.

"In the old days, we didn't need Rangers to tell us what was happening. We'd have messengers running along the Underway from Hold to Hold, telling folks what was going on, if the Orcs was on the move or whatever. Sneaking about in the rocks and woods, spying and watching, that sounds like something an Elf would do, no offence to you lad. I guess we needs to know what's going on, and who's going where and what not, but I don't envy you having to spend all that time in the open air; it'll stunt your beard, so it will."

Rangers watch over the mountain passes that snake their way through the Dwarf realms. They keep watch for approaching danger and hunt down Goblins and Orcs. When they spot an approaching army they will send signals to the watch posts of the stronghold, and, once their Karak has been warned, they will gather together at an elected meeting place. Once all their number have arrived, they get into battle formation and hound the invading army.

RANGERS

	M	WS	BS	S	T	W	I	A	Ld
Ranger	3	4	3	3	4	1	2	1	9
Veteran	3	4	3	3	4	1	2	2	9

Special Rules

Foresters. Rangers suffer no movement penalties when moving through wooded terrain.

Scouts. Rangers are scouts (see page 112 of the Warhammer rulebook).

MINERS

As he wandered back to the tavern's bar, Redmane's eye fell upon a pile of shovels and picks carefully piled up at the end of the counter.

"Some of you young 'uns work down in mines?" he asked, answered with a few cautious nods from the young Dwarfs who were slouched drunkenly at the main trestle.

"Good!" he boomed, a wide grin splitting his face. "Mining, that's a proper Dwarf job, none of this messing about with Grungni knows what. Just good honest stone and metal, that's a miner's work. Still, the mines aren't what they used to be," he continued, followed by the sound of the other Dwarfs' heads thudding to the table. "There was a time when you couldn't dig more'n a few inches without finding a nugget of gold or a seam of iron ore. Not like the mountains these days, they've swallowed it all up, so you have to grub for weeks just to find a bit of dull copper. And no one these days knows the tunnels like the old mine masters used to. Could go anywhere for a month without ever setting foot in the daylight, as it should be. A few of the old-timers, proper miners to my mind, know the secret ins and outs of the caverns around abouts, but was a time when you could ask a miner in Zhufbar about the digs in Karak Zorn and he could draw you a map from memory. Still, you lads know how to swing a pick, I trust, whether it's for a piece of gold or at a damned Elf's head."

Dwarfs have an insatiable thirst for gold, and construct deep shafts into the heart of the mountains in their quest to acquire the valuable metal. They also mine for ores and gemstones, and are very skilled at digging tunnels at incredible speed. The networks of mines and tunnels run through every mountain range. In battle, they use their knowledge of the tunnels and mastery of the pick axe with deadly intent.

MINERS

	M	WS	BS	S	T	W	I	A	Ld
Miner	3	4	3	3	4	1	2	1	9
Prospector	3	4	3	3	4	1	2	2	9

Special Rules

Underground Advance. Miners are famous for using their extensive knowledge of underground tunnels to make their way to the enemy's rear and turn up on the battlefield from a completely unexpected direction.

Miners do not have to be deployed on the table at the beginning of the battle.

Instead, starting from turn two, at the beginning of every Dwarf turn roll a dice: on a 4+ the Miners will arrive. For every successive turn after the second, add a further +1 to the roll, so they arrive on a 3+ in turn three, and so on (but an unmodified roll of 1 is always a failure).

In the Movement phase of the turn when they arrive, Miners can enter the battlefield from any table edge and will be treated exactly like a unit that has pursued an enemy off the table in the previous turn (see page 76 of the Warhammer rulebook). If the Miners fail to turn up for the entire game, they have obviously got lost in the tunnels, but their points value are not awarded to the opponent.

HAMMERERS

Durgrim Redmane paused in his storytelling long enough for a young barmaid to bring him yet another tankard of beer. Pouring the contents of the vessel down his throat in a matter of seconds he thanked the young Dwarf with a curt nod.

"How do you get to become a Hammerer sir, if it's not too presumptuous of me to ask." Handing the empty tankard back to the serving girl he motioned for her to fill it again. "Through hard work, skill and much practice, like any good warrior will tell you. There ain't no short cuts, only quick deaths." The old Dwarf's mood had become sullen and sombre. Dwarfs never took talk of battle lightly. For Dwarfs, battle was a necessary evil which had taken a heavy toll on their race after many years of long protracted warfare.

"It's my kin that've been responsible for the Hammerers being the bodyguard of the Dwarf Lords to this very day." A few of the younger Dwarfs murmured to themselves. Old Redmane was renowned for his outlandish tales but this was an extravagant claim indeed. One look at the scowling face of the old Dwarf was enough to shut them up.

"As I was saying, 'twas my great-great-great-great-great-grandfather, no less than Kadrin Redmane himself. In those days he was working as a master craftsman in the forges at the gold mines of Gunbad. King Morgrim Blackbeard had decided to pay the mines a visit to bolster morale after years of vicious fighting. As cruel fate would have it 'twas that same day that the accursed Night Goblins broke through the mine's walls. The King was at their mercy, for his small bodyguard were overwhelmed as hundreds of gibbering Grobi poured into the mines. As the last of the King's bodyguard fell, Kadrin Redmane, seeing the desperate situation, took the hammer that he had been using to work the gold and charged out of the forge to protect his liege. Seeing his brave act, the other smiths followed him. Grabbing their forge hammers, slowly they cleared an escape route out from the mines." Durgrim by now had silenced the youngsters in the crowd. Every Dwarf in the tavern was engrossed in the story.

"As a reward, the King presented Kadrin with a magnificent rune-hammer."

An overenthusiastic young Dwarf couldn't keep his excitement in check and spoke out of turn. "Was that the same hammer that he threw into Black Water to prevent it getting into Orc hands?"

Durgrim reached down to his belt and pulled out his own hammer. Intricately carved runes were inscribed upon it. Rainbows of colour danced around the room as the light of the candles reflected through the perfect prisms of the multifaceted gem fixed into the metal. "So legend would have you believe." The old Dwarf slowly rose from his stool. Tucking his hammer back into his belt, he picked up an old worn cloak and stepped out of the tavern. He turned at the door and gave one last piece of advice. "One thing you'll learn as you grow older. Don't believe all that you hear."

The Hammerers are the King's personal guard and so are accorded a high status within the stronghold. They are very skilled warriors and are personally selected by the King himself. If a Dwarf should prove himself courageous enough over the course of many battles he may be selected to join the Hammerers.

HAMMERERS

	M	WS	BS	S	T	W	I	A	Ld
Hammerer	3	5	3	4	4	1	2	1	9
Gate Keeper	3	5	3	4	4	1	2	2	9

Special Rules

Bodyguard. As long as the army's General is with the unit, Hammerers are *stubborn* (see page 85 of the Warhammer rulebook).

IRONBREAKERS

"Down in the mines, that can be dangerous work," Durgrim expounded, waving a tankard as he strolled back into the tavern, heading straight for the bar. "Not as dangerous as it used to be, mind, but then that's why our ancestors formed the Ironbreakers. Head to foot in the best gromril armour, it'd be a brave Goblin, Troll or ratman who faces an Ironbreaker and doesn't turn tail. And even if the roof caved in, not that a good proper Dwarf roof would do that, but them Goblin tunnels is shoddy work, nine times out of ten he'd climb out again, dust himself down and get back to the fight, not like you young whelps..."

The Ironbreakers guard the deep abandoned tunnels from the numerous dark creatures that would otherwise invade the hold. They spend much of their time below ground in the deepest, least visited parts of the stronghold. Because of the extreme danger of their duty they wear fine suits of gromril armour to protect themselves.

IRONBREAKERS

	M	WS	BS	S	T	W	I	A	Ld
Ironbreaker	3	5	3	4	4	1	2	1	9
Ironbeard	3	5	3	4	4	1	2	2	9

LONGBEARDS

The old Hammerer stroked a hand through his beard. "Course, if I weren't a Hammerer, I'd be with the Longbeards these days," he announced to the occupants of the smoky tavern. "When you've got proper beards you might understand what a bit of gnollengrom means, what it's like to respect a Dwarf for the fullness of his beard. This beard here says I'm old, and that means I knows best, and you knows that too, so that's why you're going listen to my advice, then you can grow up to be proper Dwarfs and pass on your advice to the next generation. Remember, a Dwarf's only as big as his beard."

Dwarfs are taught from an early age to respect their elders, and the oldest Dwarfs in the stronghold are accorded the greatest respect. Their beards must stretch down to the floor before they are given the prestigous title of Longbeard. The ceremony that follows when a Dwarf finally joins this elite caste is a great occasion; many a tavern has been drunk dry in the ensuing feast.

LONGBEARDS

	M	WS	BS	S	T	W	I	A	Ld
Longbeard	3	5	3	4	4	1	2	1	9
Greatbeard	3	5	3	4	4	1	2	2	9

Special Rules
Immune to Panic. Longbeards expect the worst, and spend a long time grumbling about the inadequacies of Dwarfs/weapons/Goblins these days, as they're not as brave/well made/scary as they were in the olden days. It takes a lot to unsettle a Longbeard from a good grumble. Longbeards automatically pass any Panic tests they have to take.

ENGINEERS GUILD

"If somebody would care to refresh my palate then perhaps I can continue." Old Redbeard, as he was more commonly known amongst the Dwarfs that frequented the Black Dragon Tavern, had emptied yet another keg of Bugman's ale. Unlike many of the younger Dwarfs who were currently collapsed asleep on the tables, he was showing little if any sign of intoxication. His red, bulbous nose was a clear indicator that he was a seasoned veteran to drink.

"Back when I were a lad, any elder recounting tales of the past would have filled this bar twice over with people, all eager to hear his words of wisdom to pass down to their children." Durgrim took the freshly filled tankard off the barman, thanking him politely.

"Still, what with all those newfangled contraptions such as the likes of Gyrocannons and Flamecopters it's hardly surprising that your generation has the attention span of a Troll. I remember my great grandfather telling me about the day the Engineers discovered blackpowder. Now I'm not one to belittle the Engineers Guild, even if they are a bunch of dangerously insane lunatics, but there are Dwarfs amongst them that'll have you believe that the invention of blackpowder was quite intentional." Durgrim chuckled to himself, *"You try telling that to the poor Dwarfs who found themselves blown straight up to the cavern roof. It took them days to clear up the mess. There's still a dent or two in the ceiling so they say."*

A few of the crowd that had gathered burst out in laughter. *"Still, for all their bumbling about they certainly know how to make good cannons. You'll rarely see a Dwarf cannon blow up, not like those shoddy, cheap, oversized pop guns that the men of the Empire are so proud of. Great Cannon, bah!"* Durgrim spat his contempt *"The only thing great 'bout them is that 'twere a Dwarf who invented 'em. Dwarf cannons are built to last. We won't even consider taking one to battle unless it's over five hundred years old. Unless the Engineer who built it has a beard down past his boots the cannon ain't worth the iron it's forged from. You see, an Engineer has to be that old to be able to help the Runesmith inscribe the correct runes. Still I reckon we'll live to regret the day that we gave the secret of blackpowder to the Manlings. It won't be long before it's turned against its creators."*

The audience murmured in general agreement with Old Redmane.

"Mind you, I still can't see them becoming too popular, there ain't nowt a cannon can do, that a determined Dwarf with a hammer can't achieve."

DWARF ARTILLERY

Dwarf armies can include Cannons, Stone Throwers and Bolt Throwers. These follow the rules given on pages 118-125 of the Warhammer rulebook. Note that a Dwarf cannon is the smaller of the two included on page 123.

ENGINEERS

"The Engineers Guild, they calls themselves," Redmane snorted. *"Messing about with blackpowder and whatnots is what I calls it. Still, them Engineers can cast a good cannon, and they know how they work like no one else. You want to land a shot on a Goblin a mile away, ask an Engineer to lay the gun for you, and he'll ask you which eye you want to hit."*

If a Dwarf shows a particular aptitude with machinery, he may be granted an apprenticeship within the Engineers Guild which maintains the numerous working devices of the Dwarfs. Guild members spend much of their time repairing broken components and cursing the shoddy work of the engineer who first constructed it. They are also responsible for inventing new devices. If the Guild thinks a concept is worthy enough it will fund the Dwarf with all the equipment, materials and help needed. Most inventions never quite take off, but others, such as the legendary Gyrocopter, quite literally do.

ENGINEERS

	M	WS	BS	S	T	W	I	A	Ld
Engineer	3	4	4	3	4	2	2	1	9

Special Rules

Artillery Master. A Cannon or a Stone Thrower (but not a Flame Cannon) which has been joined by an Engineer may make two guesses when declaring the range they are firing at (one for the crew, one for the Engineer). Measure the two points you have guessed and then decide which one you want to use for that shot before rolling any dice.

A Bolt Thrower which has been joined by an Engineer may re-roll failed rolls to hit.

Note that if the Engineer uses his ability during the firing of the war machine, he will not be able to shoot with his own missile weapon in the same Shooting phase (he is too busy grumbling about the crew's poor aim). Remember that you must fire all the weapons requiring you to guess the range before any normal shooting. In addition, you must remember to fire a Bolt Thrower which an Engineer has joined before he opens fire with his own weapon. If you fired the Engineer's own weapon then you cannot use his re-roll ability in the same turn.

When firing his own missile weapon, an Engineer can always choose a different target from the one fired upon by the machine he has joined.

Extra Crewman. An Engineer can also replace a lost crew member of a machine he joins (including Flame Cannons and Organ Guns), but if he is operating the machine, the Engineer cannot fire his own missile weapon.

If a machine with an Engineer attached to it misfires and explodes, the Engineer will be killed with the rest of the crew if he replaced a crewman or used his Artillery Master ability during that turn.

FLAME CANNON

"Now, something half decent that the Engineers have given us, though still a new gizmo in anyone's books, is the Flame Cannon," Durgrim informed his dazed audience. "One of them tried to explain to me how it works once. He said a volatile concoction of hot oil and molten tar is mixed in the barrel of the Flame Cannon. He told me air is pumped into the barrel until the pressure inside is very great and the barrel is almost ready to burst. At precisely the right moment, the crew place a burning oily wad into the nozzle and release the pressure inside. The mixture catches fire as it spurts from the barrel and burning oil arcs into the air towards the enemy ranks. With a bit of luck, the flaming oil lands right in the middle of the enemy, spraying fire and boiling tar over the target. Well, that's how they say. To me, it goes whoosh, there's a huge blast of flame, then the enemy goes running off with smoke trailing from 'em."

The Flame Cannon is a deadly weapon capable of inflicting extreme damage at short ranges. It is a brave Dwarf who volunteers to crew this extraordinary cannon, as there is a strong chance that when the flammable concoction is set alight the cannon will instantaneously explode.

Firing the Flame Cannon

Flame Cannons shoot in a similar way to cannons, but instead of firing a cannon ball they shoot a gout of flame – use the Flame template to represent this.

To fire the cannon, first turn it on the spot so that it points at your intended target. Now declare how far you wish to shoot, up to a maximum of 12", eg, 12", 10", 8", etc. This represents the gunners elevating the barrel to get the required trajectory. The jet of inflammable liquid will travel the distance you have nominated plus the score of an Artillery dice (marked 2, 4, 6, 8, 10 and Misfire).

Roll the Artillery dice and add the score to the distance you have nominated. The jet travels the total distance and will land short, hit the target, or pass over it depending on how accurately you have guessed the range and what effect the dice roll has.

Damage

When you have established where the jet of flaming liquid hits the ground, place a marker on that spot. The jet sprays out from this point and scorches a line through any targets in its way. To determine the swathe cut by the burning liquid place the Flame template with the narrow end on the point where the jet hit the ground and the wide end pointing directly away from the cannon so that the flame continues in a straight line. Any models completely under the template are automatically hit and models partially covered are hit on the roll of a 4+. Any model struck by the flame takes a Strength 5 hit and any model wounded by the flame takes D3 wounds. Saving throws apply as normal (ie, -2 armour save).

A unit which suffers casualties from the Flame Cannon must take an immediate Panic test to represent the horrific effects of this weapon.

If you roll a Misfire on the Artillery dice then the Flame Cannon has malfunctioned. Roll a D6 and check the Flame Cannon Misfire chart below to see what happens.

Profiles

Max.Range	Strength	Wounds	Armour Save
12"	5	D3	-2

You can move the Flame Cannon at the same rate as its crew, assuming they are all alive. If any crew are slain, the Move rate is reduced proportionately. The Flame Cannon may be turned on the spot to face its target, but cannot otherwise move and fire in the same turn.

Move	Toughness	Wounds
As crew	7	3

The Flame Cannon is a large and well constructed device, but by its very nature is vulnerable: all the hot tar, oil, high pressure and flame is a recipe for disaster. The Flame Cannon itself is reasonably sturdy, but if it suffers damage it becomes unreliable and dangerous. For each wound suffered by the Flame Cannon, deduct -1 on the Misfire chart for all Misfire rolls. This means that a Flame Cannon with two wounds left would deduct -1 from a roll on the Misfire chart, and any roll of a 1-3 would therefore destroy it. Suffering wounds does not increase the likelihood of a misfire, but it does make misfires more dangerous when they happen.

Loss of crew

The Flame Cannon requires a full crew of three Dwarfs to work it properly: to pump up the pressure, aim the gun, fire the nozzle, etc. If one crewman is slain the remaining pair can just about cope without slowing down the rate of work. No penalty is therefore imposed for the loss of one crewman. If two crewmen are slain, the remaining crewman won't be able to prepare the weapon properly, ie, the Flame Cannon can only be fired every other turn. Should all the crew be slain, the Flame Cannon is useless.

FLAME CANNON MISFIRE CHART

D6 Result

1-2 Destroyed! Smoke begins to pour from the barrel in a worrying fashion and a few seconds later it explodes into a fireball, engulfing everyone nearby. The Flame Cannon is destroyed and the crew slain.

3-4 Malfunction. The mixture fails to ignite and the cannon squirts smelly hot oil and tar into the air. Although unpleasant, this is not deadly, and has no effect on the target. The crew must prepare the cannon for firing again, so the Flame Cannon may not shoot this turn or next turn.

5-6 Phut. The pressure is not high enough, so the Flame Cannon may not fire this turn.

DWARF ORGAN GUN

"There was this Engineer only a few hundred years ago, Lokri Snarrison, who had this real ear for music," Redmane the Hammerer told the patrons of the tavern. *"He had this idea of some kind of big instrument that used pressure and pipes to make different noises. Anyways, he called it an organ and it sounded terrible. However, another Engineer, Durin Kurganssonson, had an idea and took all those pipes, laid 'em flat and made a big multi-barreled cannon out of them. The Organ Gun he called it, and a few other Engineers liked it so much they copied it."* He took a swig of ale to clear his throat. *"Still, them pipes weren't big enough for cannon balls, but then putting five of them together means you can fire all of the barrels at the same time, and mighty devastating it is, if it hits. Not like a proper cannon that you can train and elevate and actually aim proper, but you gets lucky every once in a while and you'll see chariots disappear into firewood and minotaurs spattered across the grass."*

One of the Engineer Guilds' stranger creations, the Organ Gun has been known to decimate entire regiments that have been foolish enough to stand before it. Whilst not as powerful as a cannon, in the right hands it can prove just as effective.

ORGAN GUN MISFIRE CHART

D6	Result
1-2	**Destroyed!** The gun explodes with a mighty crack. Shards of metal and wood fly in all directions leaving a hole in the ground, a cloud of black smoke and the stench of burnt beards. The gun is destroyed and its crew slain or injured. Remove the Organ Gun and its crew.
3-4	**Malfunction.** The gun fails to ignite and does not fire. The crew fuss around, banging it with hammers and muttering to themselves before working out what is wrong. The gun cannot fire this turn or next turn.
5-6	**Fzzz... Clunk.** A minor fault prevents the gun firing. Perhaps the fuse is not set properly or maybe the young crew mishandled the loading procedure. The Organ Gun does not shoot this turn. However, it is unharmed and may shoot as normal next turn.

Firing the Dwarf Organ Gun

In the Shooting phase, turn the Organ Gun so that it faces its target. Roll the Artillery dice and then measure the range. If the target unit is within range it will suffer a number of hits equal to the number rolled on the Artillery dice. Hits are resolved using the profile below.

If you roll a Misfire, the cannon has misfired and may explode. Roll a D6 and consult the Organ Gun Misfire chart above to see what happens.

Profiles

The Organ Gun has more barrels than an ordinary cannon but these are smaller and lighter. Its range and the damage it inflicts are considerably different from a cannon's.

Range	Strength	Armour Save
18"	5	-3

Organ Guns are stoutly made from iron and solid wood and can sustain considerable damage as shown on their profile below. An Organ Gun can be moved by its Dwarf crew at 3" per turn. If any crew are slain, the Move rate is reduced proportionally. The Organ Gun cannot move and shoot in the same turn, other than to pivot on the spot to face its target.

Move	Toughness	Wounds
As crew	7	3

Loss of crew

An Organ Gun requires a full crew of three Dwarfs to work it properly. If one crew member is slain, the other two can just about get by and the gun may fire as normal. If two crew are slain, the remaining crewman can still operate the weapon but it will take twice as long to reload – two turns instead of one. If all the crew are slain then the gun is useless.

GYROCOPTER

"When the Underway started cracking up under all the earthquakes and such, the Engineers found another way to get messages from one Hold to the next," Durgrim explained, resting his tankard on the head of a Dwarf who had flopped across the table next to him. "Couldn't go underground, and there was Orcs and Trolls and the like swarming everywhere so you couldn't go across ground. Some bright spark decided you could go over ground, and built the Gyrocopter. It's got big spinny blades powered by a steam engine, height of making small engine technology, one Engineer told me. And it can take off from a small space so it can buzz about the mountain tops with nary a worry about what's below."

He imitated a swooping Gyrocopter with his free hand, flitting across the table and resting on the tobacco pouch of a Dwarf sitting across from him, before returning with its cargo to his pipe.

"Then some Dwarf Lord, Thane Orgri I reckons, thought about putting a little cannon on one. The pilot, as they call the fool who flies the contraption, must be mad as a Halfling to go up there, if'n you

asks me. A Dwarf should have his feet on the ground or, more preferably, a hundred feet below it. But they're nippy little beggars, I can tell you, and useful for getting behind the enemy and givin' 'em a good wallop up the backside with that rapid-firing gun."

The brave and some would say insane pilots of these crazy contraptions gather together in their own distinct regiments. Due to the high costs, maintenance of the machines comes from the royal treasury and so this elite unit are known as the King's Flying Corps.

GYROCOPTER

	M	WS	BS	S	T	W	I	A	Ld
Gyrocopter	–	–	–	–	5	3	–	–	–
Pilot	–	4	–	3	–	–	2	1	9

Unit Strength
The Gyrocopter has a Unit Strength of 1.

Flying Machine
The Gyrocopter can, of course, fly as described on page 106 of the Warhammer rules.

Gyrocopters always end their move hovering at very low altitude, and may be charged by enemy troops in the same way as flying creatures. If the Gyrocopter can't fly for any reason, it can't move. If a Gyrocopter has to flee when it cannot fly, it will be removed and counts as destroyed (but won't crash). Note that the Gyrocopter does not suffer the -1 penalty to its pursuit and flee moves and so will travel the full 3D6 inches.

Steam Gun
The Gyrocopter is armed with a steam-powered gun that unleashes a hail of lead bullets similar to a cannon's grapeshot. To represent the blast of the steam gun, use the Flame template. Place the template with the broad end over the target and the narrow end touching the muzzle of the gun. Any models completely under the template are automatically hit and models partially covered are hit on the roll of a 4+.

Profile

	Range	Strength	Armour Save
Steam Gun	Flame Template	3	-1

Damage to Gyrocopters
Close combat is conducted as normal with a few exceptions. If a Gyrocopter is broken in close combat then it will automatically crash. Otherwise the Gyrocopter functions normally until it has sustained three wounds, at which point it can no longer fly and crashes. If a Gyrocopter is wounded by an Attack which is Strength 7 or more, it will crash automatically.

Crashes
A Gyrocopter will crash when the machine is destroyed or if the machine is beaten in close combat. When the Gyrocopter crashes, roll the Scatter dice to determine the random direction in which it moves (if you roll a Hit, use the little arrow included in the symbol). Now roll 4D6. This is the distance in inches the Gyrocopter moves before it crashes. When it hits the ground the machine explodes, killing the pilot. Bits of Gyrocopter and the spinning blades mangle anything nearby.

To represent the explosion, place a large Blast template (5" diameter) where the Gyrocopter hits the ground. All targets under the template suffer a Strength 4 hit due to the exploding engine and debris (models partially under are hit on a 4+). Gyrocopter pilots may not crash deliberately!

DWARF ARMOURY

Dwarfs are renowned across the Old World as superb artisans and craftsmen, and were the first to discover blackpowder weapons. Even the arrogant Elves once purchased Dwarf-forged items. Each apprentice smith and artisan must undergo decades of training before he can be called a true craftsman. And only those with a century or more of experience under their belt would claim to be experts.

Coupled with this immense skill is a Dwarf's unbending sense of pride and honour. It is claimed that it is physically impossible for a Dwarf to do a shoddy job; they simply cannot bring themselves to cut corners or make compromises in quality. This ensures that any weapon that leaves the forges is of the highest quality – every detail perfected, every nut, bolt and nail lovingly crafted with individual care and scrupulous attention.

To represent their expertise and experience, certain Dwarf units are equipped with the following battle gear, as detailed in their army list entries.

The following rules for Dwarf handguns replace those for handguns given in the Warhammer rulebook.

ARMOUR

Gromril Armour

Armour made from the metal known as gromril is the toughest and most sturdy in the known world. Known variously as meteoric iron, silverstone and hammernought armour, Gromril armour is limited to wealthy Dwarfs and the elite Ironbreakers.

Rules: Gromril armour gives a 4+ armour save.

MISSILE WEAPONS

Dwarf Handgun

The handguns of Dwarf Thunderers, called dragon belchers by the more superstitious Goblin tribes, feature many improvements over the crude devices used by other races. These features include rifled barrels, finer powder grain and more reliable firing mechanisms.

Maximum Range: 24"; **Strength:** 4

Rules: Armour piercing.

Superior design: A Dwarf handgun has a +1 to hit modifier when firing at short range.

DWARF RUNES

Magic pervades the Warhammer world and permeates all things. It flows into the material realm from beyond the Chaos Wastes as an ever-shifting flux of energy. This energy can be perceived and used by the races of the Warhammer world. Some races, such as Elves and Men, can use magic to cast terrifying and destructive spells. Dwarfs, on the other hand, are extremely resistant to magic and its influence, neither perceiving its presence nor feeling its effects.

Dwarfs have learned to use the power of magic in a different way, by incorporating it into magic items such as hammers, axes and armour. The Dwarfs are the greatest and most successful of all races when it comes to making magic items. Indeed, many of the most powerful magic weapons used by Elves and Men were made by the Dwarfs using their unique skills.

A Dwarf who makes magic items is called a **Runesmith**. As Dwarfs have no direct equivalent to a Human Wizard, he is a very important individual. The Runesmiths are an ancient guild of craftsmen, and for thousands of years they have preserved the secrets of how to forge magic runes and how to make weapons, armour and other items of incredible power.

The Dwarf language is written in runes, inscriptions specifically designed to be carved in stone or engraved in metal. Magic runes are different to ordinary runes in shape and detail, but much of what makes a rune magical is how and when it is engraved. Magic runes trap magical power – their presence binds and holds magic just as a nail holds together two pieces of timber. Most simple Dwarf runes can trap weak amounts of magic if engraved in a special way, but magic runes can entrap much greater power. Such runes include the awesome master runes and certain secret runes known only to Runesmiths of the temples of Grungni, Grimnir and Valaya.

RUNIC MAGIC

Runic magic items are effectively magic items tailored to your own requirements by combining different abilities.

A Dwarf character can carry runic magic items and the total points value of these runic items is limited in the same way as normal.

It is important to remember that a runic item is no different in principle to any other magic item, and all the usual rules for magic items still apply. For example, if a creature cannot be harmed by an ordinary weapon but can be harmed by a magic weapon, then obviously a runic weapon will affect it too. All the rules that apply to the possession and use of magic items also apply to runic magic items.

CREATING A RUNE ITEM

Runes can be inscribed onto any of the following things: weapons, armour, standards, war machines and talismans. Each of these has its own type of runes.

The easiest way to create a runic item is to choose a character from your army – a Dwarf Thane armed with an axe, for example. By inscribing runes onto his axe you will be, in effect, arming him with a magic weapon – a rune-axe. You can choose which rune you want from the Weapon runes detailed in this section. Each rune has a specific points value; the more powerful the rune the higher the points cost. You can put up to three runes onto a weapon, paying the appropriate cost each time.

Once you have chosen the runes you want, write down the Thane's name on a piece of paper and note that he has a rune-axe with the runes you have selected. Note down the total points cost of the runes you have used and add this to the character's points value. You should make a list of all your characters that are using runic items so that you can refer to it during the battle. It is a good idea to make a brief note of what each rune does, as this will save you looking up details during play.

NUMBER OF RUNIC ITEMS

A character may have no more than one runic item from each of the five categories (ie, one runic weapon, one runic armour/shield, one runic talisman, etc). Remember, a character with a magic weapon can't use other weapons.

CHOOSING RUNES

There are many types of rune, all of which bestow a special power or bonus. By combining runes together in different ways, you can create devices of great power. The most powerful runes are very expensive; others are cheaper.

It is up to you to decide how to use the runes. It is the ability to tailor your magic items to your foe or to your tactics which makes runic magic items so uniquely useful.

RULE OF THE RUNES

You may inscribe up to three runes on a runic magic item, subject to the following restrictions:

1. No item can have more than three runes. It is virtually impossible to forge items able to bear the strain of carrying so much power. Runesmiths call this the **Rule of Three**.

2. Weapon runes can only be inscribed on weapons, Armour runes can only be inscribed on armour, Protection runes can only be inscribed on standards, Engineering runes can only be inscribed on war machines, and Talismanic runes can only be inscribed on talismans (of which more later). This is called the **Rule of Form** by Runesmiths. You cannot inscribe Armour runes on a cannon nor can you place Engineering runes on an axe.

3. No more than one item may carry the same combination of magic runes. You could not have a rune-hammer and a rune-axe both engraved with a Rune of Breaking and a Rune of Fire, for example. This restriction also applies to the use of single runes, so you could not have two characters in your army wearing armour engraved with a single Rune of Resistance. Creating rune items takes a great deal of effort and Runesmiths don't like repeating themselves. Nor do they copy other Runesmiths' work, except during their apprenticeship. This is known among Runesmiths as the **Rule of Pride**.

4. No master rune may be used more than once per army, and no more than one master rune can be inscribed on an item. Master runes are so powerful that they cannot be combined together on the same item or used together on the same battlefield. For this reason, Runesmiths describe these runes as **Jealous Runes**.

5. Apart from the master runes (which can only be used once) other runes can be combined as you wish to produce varied or cumulative effects. For example, you might inscribe a weapon with the Master Rune of Swiftness (always strikes first), the Rune of Striking (+1 Weapon Skill) and the Rune of Fury (+1 Attack). With the exception of master runes, runes can be used in multiples in which case their effects are added together. For example, you could inscribe a weapon with the Rune of Fury (+1 Attack) three times to give you +3 Attacks.

A RUNE RITE OF FORGING

Seek the mountain's heart.

Take it on third moon's last day.

Stoke the furnace at midnight.

When the ore glows red.

Hammer it before dawn.

Seven times bend the white hot metal upon itself.

Seven times sing the forging song.

Quench in dragon's blood.

Slake red hot in Karak Ungol's quicksilver

Do this in Haki the ancestor's name.

Temper in Varn's water.

Hone the blade upon a dragon's horn.

On winter's third moon, carve the slaying rune.

Anoint with blood of troll, slain on Grungni's day.

Bind the hilt with dragon's hide, with hornside inside.

Haft the hilt with Azgal's gold, bind with Azul-metal.

Mark the Orc's fang pommel with Grimnir's sign.

Make the naming rite with ale upon Valaya's altar.

The slaying of a troll by night will make the rune to glow.

For a thousand years.

WEAPON RUNES

Weapon runes are inscribed onto hammers or axes to turn them into runic weapons. Note that although Dwarfs may inscribe runes on weapons, none of the bonuses/penalties for the original weapon apply. The fact that the weapon is magical supersedes any normal rules for such weapons.

MASTER RUNE OF SNORRI SPANGELHELM 75 points

Runesmith to the High King in Karaz-a-Karak during the time of Kallon, Snorri wrought the exquisite war panoply of the High Kings for several generations. He fought in many battles and was renowned for his magnificent gromril armour as well as this unique weapon rune.

Any blows struck by a weapon engraved with this rune will always hit. No roll to hit is necessary.

MASTER RUNE OF SKALF BLACKHAMMER 75 points

The legendary Runesmith Skalf forged many great hammers, and some say even Sigmar's hammer was his work. Many of his hammers were later held by Dwarf Lords as heirlooms of their kingship.

Any weapon bearing this rune will automatically wound if it hits. Roll to hit as normal. No roll to wound is required. Use the character's Strength for the save modifier.

MASTER RUNE OF ALARIC THE MAD 50 points

No one knows exactly what happened to Alaric the Mad after he forged the famous Runefangs of the Elector Counts of the Empire, though some say he wrought rune weapons for the Khan Queens of Kislev.

This rune cancels an opponent's armour saving throw. When wounded by this weapon, the target is not allowed an armour saving throw of any kind.

MASTER RUNE OF FLIGHT 50 points

The original inscription for this rune did not specify that the hammer return to the wielder's hand, and many Dwarfs found themselves knocked unconscious as their own weapons returned to them.

This rune may only be inscribed onto a hammer. The hammer can be thrown at any model in sight and within 12", including models which cannot be singled out by normal shooting (like characters inside units). The target is automatically hit once as if the two models were in close combat, then the hammer flies back into the wielder's hand.

MASTER RUNE OF BREAKING 50 points

First used during the War of Vengeance, this rune was inscribed upon King Gorrin's axe, which destroyed the High Elf General Elthior's enchanted blade. It has become a popularly used rune ever since.

If the Dwarf character scores a hit against an enemy with a magic weapon, the enemy's magic weapon is destroyed immediately. Multiple runes have no further effect.

MASTER RUNE OF SWIFTNESS 25 points

First struck by Thurgrom the Hermit, the last Runesmith to work in the Elf cities of the Old World.

A weapon engraved with this rune always strikes first. In situations where both sides are entitled to strike first, the highest Initiative value has priority over the lower value. If Initiatives are equal, both sides roll a D6 and the highest score strikes first.

RUNE OF MIGHT 25 points

Though short in stature, a Dwarf using a weapon inscribed with this rune is a powerful opponent.

Double Strength against any enemies with Toughness 5 or more. Multiple runes have no further effect.

RUNE OF FURY 25 points

The Dwarf wielding the weapon must concentrate upon an unavenged grudge, causing him to become enraged at the wrongs his race have endured.

The wielder of this weapon adds +1 to his Attack characteristic.

RUNE OF CLEAVING 20 points

Originally forged upon the axes of miners, enabling them to break through the hardest rock.

The wielder of this weapon adds +1 to his Strength.

GRUDGE RUNE 15 points

Often an enemy's misdeeds are so great that a Dwarf will have this rune put upon his weapon and will not rest until his foe pays for his wrongs with blood.

Nominate one enemy character or monster at the beginning of the game. The wielder may re-roll misses in close combat when attacking this enemy model. Multiple runes of this type have no additional effect (a dice can only be re-rolled once).

RUNE OF STRIKING 10 points

The properties of this rune enable the weapon's wielder to find an enemy's weak points with ease.

The wielder of this weapon may add +1 to his Weapon Skill.

RUNE OF SPEED 5 points

This rune enhances the Dwarf's awareness.

The wielder of this weapon adds +1 to his Initiative.

RUNE OF FIRE 5 points

A skilled Runesmith is able to inscribe this rune on the metal when it is still white hot from the forge.

Flaming attacks. This can cause extra damage on some targets (such as Treemen, Mummies, etc).

"Put your trust in stone and iron – stone and iron have always been true friends of the Dwarfs."

Old Dwarf saying

ARMOUR RUNES

These runes are the most powerful protective magic known to the Dwarfs. They are inscribed on armour or shields. Any Dwarf character who has armour or a shield may be given up to three Armour runes. The maximum armour save that can be reached by combining runes, or runes and normal equipment, is 1+.

MASTER RUNE OF STEEL   75 points

Once this rune has been forged, it binds metals together making them more resilient. Armour with this rune never rusts through weathering or age.

Your opponent must re-roll successful rolls to wound against the character.

MASTER RUNE OF ADAMANT   75 point

First forged on a shield as a gift for the flamboyant Dwarf Prince Gudii Twoboots, the shield was subsequently stolen by a lone bandit who stalked the Undgrim preying on small parties of travellers.

This rune adds +1 to the Toughness of the character.

MASTER RUNE OF GROMRIL   25 points

A small amount of pure gromril is the most important element used when inscribing this rune. If the sample is even slightly flawed, the rune will not work.

Confers a 1+ armour save that cannot be improved in any way.

RUNE OF FORTITUDE   50 points

It is rumoured amongst those Dwarfs who have worn this armour that it becomes sentient. Whilst no Runesmith has ever confirmed this rumour, they make no attempts to deny it either.

This rune gives its bearer +1 Wound.

RUNE OF SHIELDING   30 points

This rune was created during the War of Vengeance as a protection against the superior missile fire of the High Elves.

The character has a 2+ Ward save against missile attacks only (including magic missiles). Multiple runes have no further effect.

RUNE OF RESISTANCE   25 points

First used on the armour of the Thane of Karak Azgal by Gorgi Strongbeard, this rune is thought to have been lost amongst the ruined stronghold. Fortunately the Runesmith survived to replicate it.

This rune allows the character to re-roll any failed armour saving throws. As you're only ever allowed one re-roll, multiples of this rune would have no effect.

RUNE OF IRON   15 points

When iron is saturated with magic it is known as lodestone. This rune focuses the magnetic properties of lodestone to create magical armour.

This rune confers a 6+ Ward save. Two of these runes confer a 5+ Ward save, but three cannot be taken, because only the Master Rune of Spite can bind such huge power.

RUNE OF STONE   5 points

Dwarf tradition tells that the ancients were created from the rock of the first mountains, so the Rune of Stone is the first rune an apprentice learns.

This rune adds +1 to the character's armour save. The Rune of Stone is an exception to the normal Rule of Pride which forbids the same combination of runes to be used on several items, so a single Rune of Stone may be inscribed onto any character's armour. The Rune of Stone is also an exception in that it cannot be used more than once on the same item, so it is not possible to give two or three Runes of Stone to the same character.

RUNIC STANDARDS

These runes may be inscribed on standards and offer the entire unit protection from psychology and magic. They may also be inscribed on the Battle Standard. Master runes are placed upon Battle Standards by the priests of the temples of Grungni, Grimnir and Valaya.

MASTER RUNE OF VALAYA   125 points

This ancient rune is said to have been invented at the dawn of time by Valaya the Ancestor Goddess.

This rune adds +2 to all attempts to dispel made by the Dwarf player. Any spell which remains in play is dispelled automatically at the start of the Magic phase if the target it affects is within 12" of the standard. For example, a Wall of Fire will be dispelled if it is within 12" of the standard.

MASTER RUNE OF STROMNI REDBEARD   100 points

Stromni Redbeard made this rune in the days of Bael, Lord of Karak Azul. It was first carved onto the battle standard of Durgin, son of Grindol, son of Grimnir.

The Battle Standard adds a further +1 to the combat result of all Dwarf units within 12" of it.

MASTER RUNE OF TAUNTING   75 points
One use only

This rune focuses the Dwarfs' ability to chant and gesticulate in such an offensive manner that they enrage the enemy beyond all self control.

Nominate one enemy unit within 12" when it is time for the enemy to declare charges. The unit must be able to charge according to the normal rules. The enemy unit must either declare a charge against the unit with the banner, or must flee in the Compulsory Movement phase as if it had failed a panic test. This rune has no effect on units that are Immune to Psychology.

MASTER RUNE OF FEAR   75 points

The clan that takes this banner to battle give the illusion that they tower over the enemy. Dwarfs are a strong enough opponent in their own right but a unit of giant Dwarfs is enough to scare even the strongest enemy.

The unit causes *fear* exactly as described in the psychology rules in the Warhammer rulebook, page 81. A unit which causes *fear* is not affected by *fear* itself.

21

MASTER RUNE OF GROTH ONE-EYE — 60 points

Groth One-Eye, famous for never backing down in an argument, struck this rune in the time of Kurgan Ironbeard when the greenskins were driven from the west.

The unit is *stubborn*.

RUNE OF COURAGE — 50 points

Resonating with the power of duty and loyalty, this rune further bolsters the resolve of Dwarfs near it.

The unit is Immune to Psychology.

RUNE OF KADRIN — 50 points

It is said that any who have undergone the pilgrimage to the shrine of Grimnir at Karak Kadrin will forever be blessed with good fortune. This rune glows bright red at the centre of the shrine and has been forged onto banners to bless them with good fortune too.

The unit re-rolls all rolls of 1 to hit when shooting and in close combat. Multiple runes have no further effect.

RUNE OF SLOWNESS — 50 points

This rune creates an almost physical barrier from the intractable nature of the Dwarfs around it.

Any foes charging the unit subtract D6" from their charge distance. If the unit fails to make contact then all the usual rules for a failed charge apply. If multiples of this rune are used, the charge reduction is not added up, instead roll a D6 for each rune and choose the best score.

RUNE OF BATTLE — 25 points

Each of the Dwarf strongholds once had a banner with the Rune of Battle upon it. Many of these banners are now lost, but those that still remain in Dwarf hands are held aloft with pride.

The unit adds a further +1 to its combat result score. A banner cannot have multiple Runes of Battle.

RUNE OF SANCTUARY — 20 points

This rune creates an area of anti-magic, using the defiance of the Dwarfs to deflect mystical attacks.

Each rune adds one dice to any dispel attempt against enemy spells cast against the unit.

ENGINEERING RUNES

Dwarf Cannons, Stone Throwers and Bolt Throwers may be inscribed with up to three of the Engineering Runes described below. The newfangled (to the Dwarfs) Organ Gun, Flame Cannon and Gyrocopter may not have Engineering runes. Note that a shot from a war machine inscribed with Engineering runes counts as a magical attack.

MASTER RUNE OF DEFENCE — 40 points

Developed as a defensive measure during the War of Vengeance against the firepower of the High Elves, this rune has saved the lives of many crew.

All incoming missiles (including *magic missiles*) hit the machine itself on a 1-5 and the crew only on a 6.

MASTER RUNE OF DISGUISE — 30 points

This rune magically distorts space around the machine, rendering it almost invisible.

Until it moves or shoots, the machine cannot be seen, and cannot therefore be targeted with spells, shot at, or charged. Once the machine has moved/fired, or if an enemy unit moves to within 3" of it, the machine is revealed and can be seen and attacked as normal for the rest of the battle.

MASTER RUNE OF IMMOLATION — 30 points

Devised to stop machines falling to the enemy, it is invoked only in desperate circumstances.

The Dwarf player can cause the machine to explode at any time. If the machine explodes, place the large circular template on the machine. The machine is destroyed and all models under the template suffer a Strength 4 hit (models partially covered are hit on the roll of a 4+).

MASTER RUNE OF SKEWERING — 25 points
One use only

Elf mages helped create this before the War of the Beard. There's no mention of this in Dwarf records.

This rune may only be inscribed on a Bolt Thrower. Once per game the Bolt Thrower hits on a 2+ with no modifiers. You must choose to use this rune before rolling to hit.

RUNE OF FORGING — 35 points

When making a cannon, with each hammer blow an Engineer strikes, a Runesmith must recite a special litany. This can take weeks to complete.

Can only be placed on a cannon. Allows Dwarf player to re-roll Artillery dice when he rolls a Misfire. If you roll a Misfire when rolling Artillery dice either to hit or to bounce, then you can roll again. You are bound by the second roll even if it's another Misfire. Multiples have no effect.

RUNE OF RELOADING — 30 points

After a cannon has proved its reliablity, a Runesmith may deem it worthy of this rune.

Cannon can shoot every turn, as long as there is at least one crewman left, even if the machine has rolled a 2-3 on the Misfire table in the previous turn. Multiples have no effect.

RUNE OF ACCURACY — 25 points

Once a missile inscribed with this rune is launched, the rune glows, invoking the winds of magic to blow the stone in the right direction.

May only be put on a Stone Thrower. The Dwarf player may re-roll the Scatter dice if he wishes, enabling the machine to shoot more accurately. If you re-roll the dice, you must accept the result of the second roll. Multiples have no effect.

RUNE OF FORTUNE — 25 points

Discovered by Magnus Hammerson, who broke Runesmith tradition by selling it to the Engineers Guild.

If a machine has the Rune of Fortune the player may re-roll a dice rolled on the machine's Misfire chart. For example, you can re-roll a result on the Cannon Misfire chart, or the Misfire chart for Stone Throwers. However, you must accept the result of the second dice roll. Multiples have no effect.

VALIANT RUNE 25 points

Dwarf crews are famed for always defending their machines to the bitter end when attacked.

As long as their war machine is not destroyed, the war machine crew are Unbreakable.

RUNE OF PENETRATING 25 points

This rune is inscribed onto the war machine's ammunition, making it more hard-hitting.

The Strength of a hit from the war machine increases by +1.

FLAKKSON'S RUNE OF SEEKING 25 points

This makes bolt throwers deadly against flyers by magically directing the bolts to their target.

Each rune adds +1 to the bolt thrower's to hit rolls against targets with the Fly special ability.

STALWART RUNE 20 points

Many Dwarfs believe that a machine with this rune on it will last forever.

This rune adds +1 to the crew's combat resolution score.

RUNE OF BURNING 5 points

Any ammunition shot by the machine bursts into flames as it hits its target.

The war engine makes flaming attacks.

RUNIC TALISMANS

Talismanic runes can be inscribed upon amulets, belts, crowns, helms and other ornamental pieces, though they are most commonly found on rings. Every character is assumed to already have the relevant item in his possession.

MASTER RUNE OF KINGSHIP 100 points

Gotrek Starbreaker was the first great Dwarf lord to have his crown adorned with this rune. Such a crown is a priceless artefact and the loss of one is dearly mourned as it absorbs the wisdom of its former master and passes this on to the next crown bearer.

This rune may only be engraved on the crown of a Dwarf Lord. The Lord and the unit he leads are *stubborn* and completely immune to *fear* and *terror*.

MASTER RUNE OF BALANCE 50 points
Runesmiths/Runelords only

Forged in the embers of a captured spell book, this rune hungers after magical power, stealing it from the enemy.

During the enemy's Magic phase, this rune allows the Dwarf player to remove one dice from the opponent's pile of Power dice and add it to his own Dispel dice pile.

MASTER RUNE OF SPELLBINDING 50 points
Runesmiths/Runelords only

This rune allows a Runesmith to channel away the winds of magic with greater ease, thwarting the magical attacks of their foes.

+1 to all attempts to dispel.

MASTER RUNE OF SPITE 45 points

Created to protect the gates of Karaz-a-Karak, this rune has since been transferred onto other devices.

This rune confers a 4+ Ward save.

MASTER RUNE OF DISMAY 40 points
One use only

When a war horn with this rune is sounded, its uncanny voice causes all foes to tremble.

The horn may be sounded once per battle, at the end of the Dwarf player's turn. All enemy units on the field which are not Immune to Psychology must take a Leadership test. If they fail, they are so dismayed that they may not declare a charge in their following turn's Movement phase. Units that move in the compulsory Movement phase are not affected.

SPELLEATER RUNE 50 points
Runesmiths/Runelords only – one use only

This rune makes Runesmiths and Runelords almost invulnerable to magical attacks.

This rune works exactly like a Rune of Spellbreaking (see below). Also, when the enemy spell is cancelled, roll a dice. On the roll of a 4+ the enemy spell is lost and can't be cast again for the rest of the game.

RUNE OF FATE 35 points
One use only

A Dwarf possessing this rune will dream portents of the future the night before a battle, and he will know each blow that the enemy will strike at him.

The model has a 2+ Ward save against the first wound suffered.

RUNE OF SPELLBREAKING 25 points
Runesmiths/Runelords only – one use only

Once a Runesmith has mastered the Rune of Warding he will learn this more complex rune.

This rune may only be used once per battle, and will stop enemy magic instantly. The rune may be played to automatically dispel one enemy spell – there is no need to roll. This rune won't help against spells cast with Irresistable Force.

RUNE OF LUCK 25 points
One use only

First inscribed on a ring worn by Magnund Hammerson, who then went on to acquire a fortune through gambling.

This rune allows its bearer to re-roll any single dice roll once during the game.

RUNE OF WARDING 20 points

Apprentice Runesmiths are taught the techniques necessary to create this rune early in their studies.

This rune adds a dice to any attempt to dispel enemy spells cast against the character or the unit he is with.

RUNE OF THE FURNACE 5 points

Designed to aid Dwarfs working in the hot forges, this rune was soon adapted for use in battle.

The bearer of this rune is immune to fire and cannot be affected by fire attacks (including magical fire, the flames of a Skaven warpfire thrower, etc).

FORCES OF THE DWARFS

The purpose of an army list is to enable players with vastly different armies to stage games which are as fair and as evenly balanced as it is possible to make them. The army list gives each individual model a points value which represents its capabilities on the tabletop. The higher a model's points value the better it is in one or more respects: stronger, tougher, faster, better leadership, and so on. The value of the army is simply the value of all the models added together.

As well as providing points costs, the list divides the army into its constituent units and describes the weapons and optional equipment that troops can have and occasionally restricts the number of very powerful units an army can include. It would be very silly indeed if an army were to consist entirely of thundering cannons, or crazed Daemon Slayers. The resultant game would be a frustrating and unbalanced affair if not a complete waste of time. We employ army lists to ensure that this does not happen!

HOW THE ARMY LIST IS INTENDED TO BE USED

The army lists enable two players to choose armies of equal points value to fight a battle, as described in the main body of the Warhammer rules. The following list has been constructed with this purpose in mind.

The list can also be used when playing specific scenarios, either those described in the Warhammer rulebook, or others, including ones invented by the players. In this case, the list provides a framework which the players can adapt as required. It might, for example, be felt necessary to increase or decrease the number of characters or units allowed, or to restrict or remove options in the standard list such as certain runes or specific weapons. If you refer to the Scenarios section of the Warhammer rulebook (pages 196-213), you'll find some examples of this kind.

ARMY LIST ORGANISATION

The army list is divided into four sections:

CHARACTERS
Representing the most able, skilled and ancient individuals in your army, characters are extraordinary leaders such as Thanes and Runesmiths. These form a vital and potent part of your forces.

CORE UNITS
These represent the most common warriors. They usually form the bulk of the army and will often bear the brunt of the fighting.

SPECIAL UNITS
This category includes the best of your warriors and common engines of war. They are available to your army in limited numbers.

RARE UNITS
So called because they are scarce compared to your ordinary troops. They represent unique units, uncommon creatures and unusual machines.

CHOOSING AN ARMY

Both players choose armies to the same agreed points value. Most players find that 2,000 points is about right for a battle that will last over an evening. Whatever value you agree, this is the maximum number of points you can spend on your army. You can spend less and will probably find it is impossible to use up every last point. Most 2,000 points armies will therefore be something like 1,998 points or 1,999 points, but they still count as '2,000' points armies for our purposes.

Once you have decided on a total points value it is time to choose your force.

Choosing Characters

Characters are divided into two broad categories: Lords (the most powerful characters) and Heroes (the rest). The maximum number of characters an army can include is shown on the chart below.

Army Points Value	Max. Total Characters	Max. Lords	Max. Heroes
Less than 2,000	3	0	3
2,000 or more	4	1	4
3,000 or more	6	2	6
4,000 or more	8	3	8
Each +1,000	+2	+1	+2

An army does not have to include the maximum number of characters allowed, it can always include fewer than indicated. **However, an army must always include at least one character: the General.** An army does not have to include Lords – it can include all of its characters as Heroes if you prefer. At the beginning of the battle, choose one of the characters to be the General and make sure that you let your opponent know which one it is.

For example, a 2,500 points army could include a Runelord (Lord), a Thane (Hero), a Runesmith (Hero), and a Dragon Slayer (Hero) (ie, four characters in total, of which one is a Lord).

Choosing Troops

Troops are divided into Core, Special and Rare Units. The number of each type of unit available depends on the army's points value, indicated on the chart below.

Army Points Value	Core Units	Special Units	Rare Units
Less than 2,000	2+	0-3	0-1
2,000 or more	3+	0-4	0-2
3,000 or more	4+	0-5	0-3
4,000 or more	5+	0-6	0-4
Each +1,000	+1 minimum	+0-1	+0-1

In some cases other limitations may apply to a particular kind of unit. This is specified in the unit entry. For example, the Hammerers Special Unit entry is accompanied by a note explaining that a maximum of one unit of this kind can be included in the army.

Unit Entries

Each unit is represented by an entry in the army list. The unit's name is given and any limitations that apply are explained.

Profiles. The characteristic profiles for the troops in each unit are given in the unit entry. Where several profiles are required, these are also given even if, as in many cases, they are optional.

Unit Sizes. Each entry specifies the minimum size for each unit. In the case of Core Units this is usually 10 models. In the case of other units it is usually less. There are exceptions as you will see. In some cases, units also have a maximum size.

Weapons and Armour. Each entry lists the standard weapons and armour for that unit type. The value of these items is included in the points value. Additional or optional weapons and armour cost extra and are covered in the Options section of the unit entry.

Options. Many entries list the different weapon, armour and equipment options for the unit and any additional points cost for taking them. It may also include the option to upgrade a unit member into a Champion. While this model usually has a specific name (the Champion of a Miner unit is called a Prospector, for example) all the rules that apply to Champions apply to them. See the appropriate section of the Warhammer Rulebook for details (pages 108-109).

Special Rules. Many troops have special rules, which are fully described elsewhere in this book. These rules are also summarised for your convenience in the army list.

It would be a long and tedious business to repeat all the special rules for every unit within the army list itself. The army list is intended primarily as a tool for choosing armies rather than for presenting game rules. Wherever possible we have indicated where special rules apply and, where space permits, we have provided notes within the list as 'memory joggers'. Bear in mind that these descriptions are not necessarily exhaustive or definitive and players should refer to the main Warhammer rulebook for a full account.

Dogs of War

Dogs of War are troops of other races who are prepared to fight under your flag in return for money, food, or some other suitable reward. A selection of such regiments are available as part of the Dogs of War range of models. The option to include Dogs of War units is included in the army list as part of the Rare Units section.

Some players prefer to play without Dogs of War – choosing to field armies of pure and noble purpose unsullied by grubby financial transactions. If both players prefer to field armies without Dogs of War then they are free to agree before the battle not to employ untrustworthy sell-swords.

Conversely, if players wish to add more colour and variety to their armies then they may wish to employ more of these spectacular units. If both players agree before the battle then Dogs of War units can be included as Special Unit choices as well as Rare Unit choices.

LORDS

Dwarf Lords (Lords, Runelords and Daemon Slayers) are the most ancient and powerful characters in the Dwarf list.

Dwarf Lords are limited in number and expensive, but make the best army Generals.

Remember that Dwarf Lords all bear the Ancestral Grudge and are also Relentless (See page 6).

† 0-1 ANVIL OF DOOM

A Runelord can bring into battle the holy Anvil of Doom accompanied by two Anvil Guards (see pages 8-9 of this army book).

	M	WS	BS	S	T	W	I	A	Ld
Anvil Guard	3	5	3	4	4	1	2	2	10

Equipment
Hand weapon, gromril armour & shield.

LORD — Points/model: 135

	M	WS	BS	S	T	W	I	A	Ld
Lord	3	7	4	4	5	3	4	4	10

Weapons: Hand weapon.

Options:
- May choose either a Great Weapon (+6 pts), or a pistol (+10 pts).
- May also choose either a crossbow (+15 pts), or a Dwarf handgun (+21 pts).
- May wear either light armour (+3 pts), heavy armour (+6 pts), or gromril armour (+12 pts), and may also carry a shield (+3 pts).
- May choose runic items from the Weapons, Armour and Talisman lists (pages 20-23), with a maximum total value of 125 pts.

RUNELORD† — Points/model: 140

	M	WS	BS	S	T	W	I	A	Ld
Rune Lord	3	6	4	4	5	3	3	2	10

Weapons: Hand weapon.

Options:
- May be armed with a Great Weapon (+6 pts).
- May wear either light armour (+3 pts), heavy armour (+6 pts), or gromril armour (+12 pts), and may also carry a shield (+3 pts).
- May bring an Anvil of Doom to battle (+200 pts). If he does so, he can't choose any extra weapons from the lists above. The Anvil of Doom comes with two Anvil Guards equipped with hand weapon, gromril armour and shield.
- May choose runic items from the Weapons, Armour and Talisman lists (pages 20-23), with a maximum total value of 150 pts.

Special Rules
Adds 1 dice to the Dispel pool (see the Warhammer rulebook, p.136).

DAEMON SLAYER — Points/model: 130

	M	WS	BS	S	T	W	I	A	Ld
Daemon Slayer	3	7	3	4	5	3	5	4	10

Weapons: Hand weapon.

Options:
- May choose either a Great Weapon (+6 pts), or an additional hand weapon (+6 pts).
- May choose runic items from the Weapons lists (page 20), with a maximum total value of 100 pts.

Special Rules
Slayer; Unbreakable; Loner (see page 7).

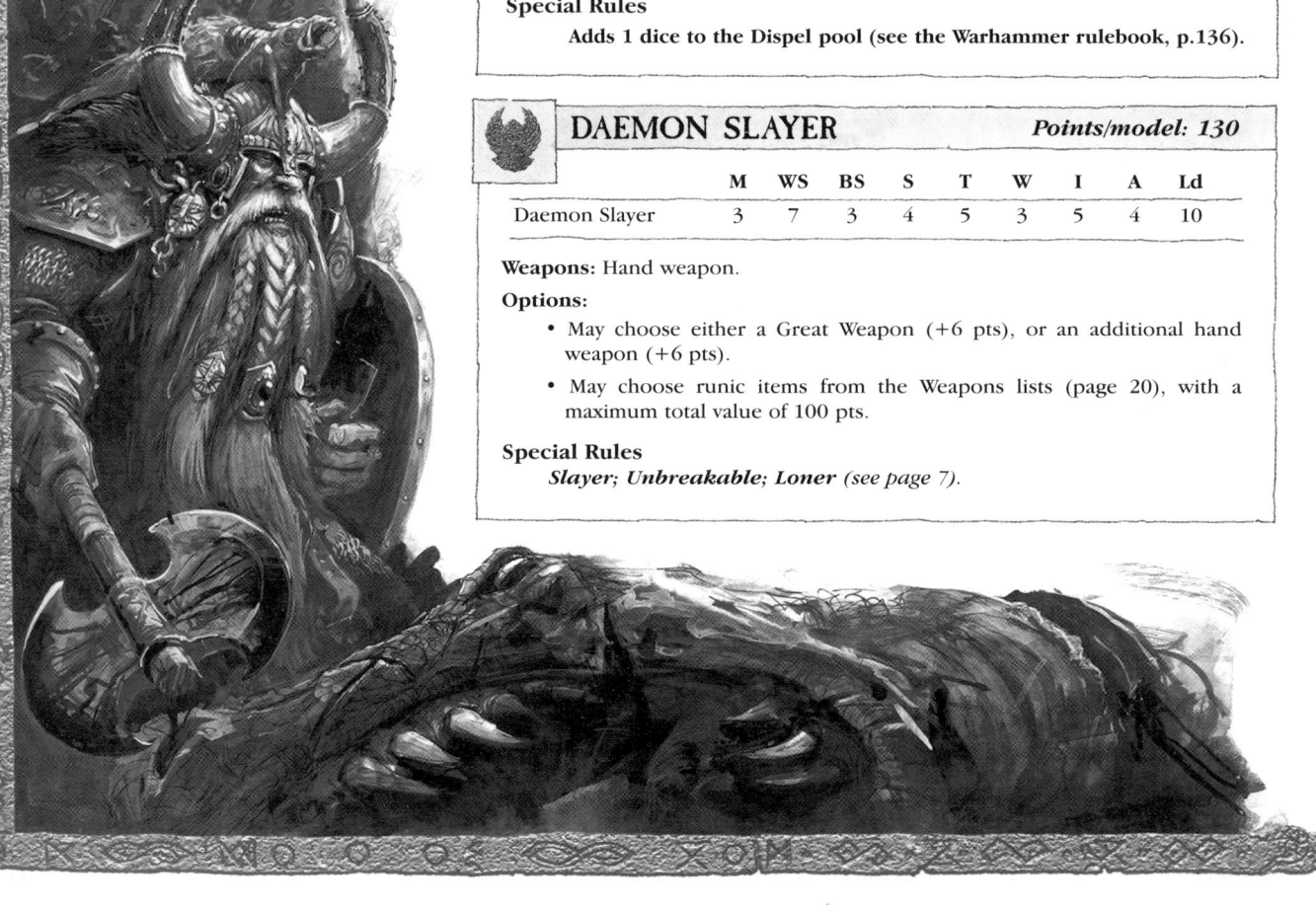

THANE*
Points/model: 55

	M	WS	BS	S	T	W	I	A	Ld
Thane	3	6	4	4	4	2	3	3	9

Weapons: Hand weapon.
Options:
- May choose either a Great Weapon (+4 pts), or a pistol (+7 pts).
- May also choose either a crossbow (+10 pts), or a Dwarf handgun (+14 pts).
- May wear either light armour (+2 pts), heavy armour (+4 pts), or gromril armour (+8 pts), and may also carry a shield (+2 pts).
- May choose runic items from the Weapons, Armour and Talisman lists (pages 20-23), with a maximum total value of 50 pts.

RUNESMITH
Points/model: 70

	M	WS	BS	S	T	W	I	A	Ld
Runesmith	3	5	4	4	4	2	2	2	9

Weapons: Hand weapon.
Options:
- May be armed with a Great Weapon (+4 pts).
- May wear either light armour (+2 pts), heavy armour (+4 pts), or gromril armour (+8 pts), and may also carry a shield (+2 pts).
- May choose runic items from the Weapons, Armour and Talisman lists (pages 20-23), with a maximum total value of 75 pts.

Special Rules
Adds 1 dice to the Dispel pool (see the Warhammer rulebook, p.136).

ENGINEER
Points/model: 65

	M	WS	BS	S	T	W	I	A	Ld
Engineer	3	4	4	3	4	2	2	1	9

Weapons: Hand weapon.
Options:
- May choose either a Great Weapon (+4 pts), a pistol (+7 pts) or a brace of pistols (two pistols, +14 pts).
- May also choose a Dwarf handgun (+14 pts).
- May wear either light armour (+2 pts), heavy armour (+4 pts), or gromril armour (+8 pts).
- May choose runic items from the Weapons, Armour and Talisman lists (pages 20-23), with a maximum total value of 50 pts.

Special Rules
Artillery Master; Extra Crewman (See page 14).

DRAGON SLAYER
Points/model: 65

	M	WS	BS	S	T	W	I	A	Ld
Dragon Slayer	3	6	3	4	4	2	4	3	10

Weapons: Hand weapon.
Options:
- May choose either a Great Weapon (+4 pts), or an additional hand weapon (+4 pts).
- May choose runic items from the Weapons lists (pages 20-23), with a maximum total value of 50 pts.

Special Rules
Slayer; Unbreakable; Loner (See page 7).

HEROES

Heroes (Thanes, Runesmiths, Engineers and Dragon Slayers) are the bravest Dwarf warriors in the army, so make great leaders.

The total number of characters you can field in your army can be found on page 25.

Remember that Dwarf Heroes bear the Ancestral Grudge and are also Relentless (See page 6).

*ARMY BATTLE STANDARD

One Thane in the army may carry the Battle Standard for +25 pts.

This Thane cannot be the army's General even if he has the highest Leadership value in the army.

The Thane carrying the Battle Standard cannot choose any extra weapons, nor can he use a shield.

If a Thane is carrying the Battle Standard, he can have any runic banner (no points limit), but if he carries a runic banner he cannot carry any other runic item.

CORE UNITS

Core Units are the most common warriors in the army. There is a minimum number of Core Units that must be fielded, depending on the size of the army.

There is no maximum limit on the amount of Core Units that can be fielded.

On this page are listed the Dwarf units that are regarded as forming the backbone of the Dwarfs' strongholds.

All Dwarfs bear the Ancestral Grudge and are Relentless and Resolute (See page 6 for rules).

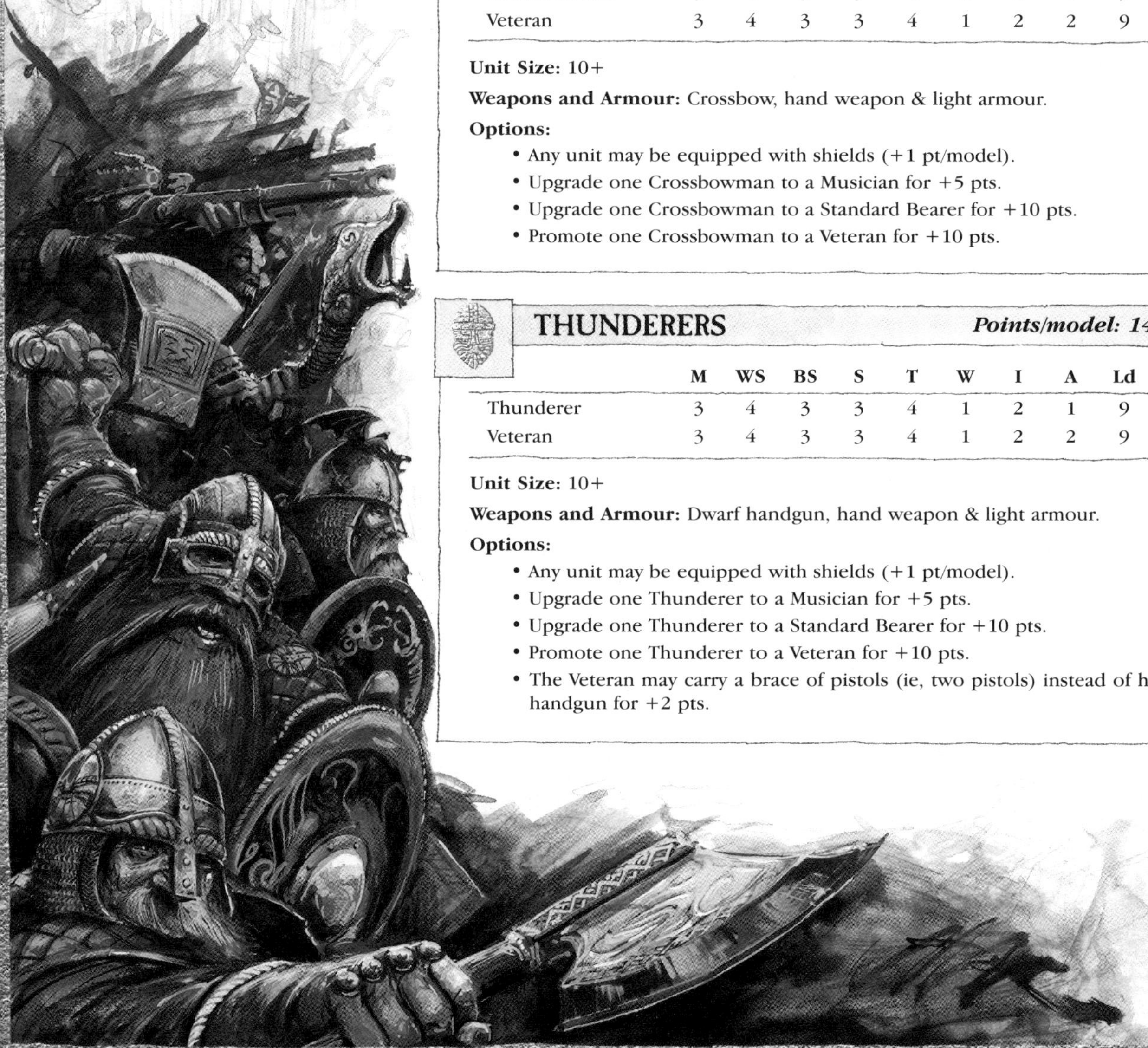

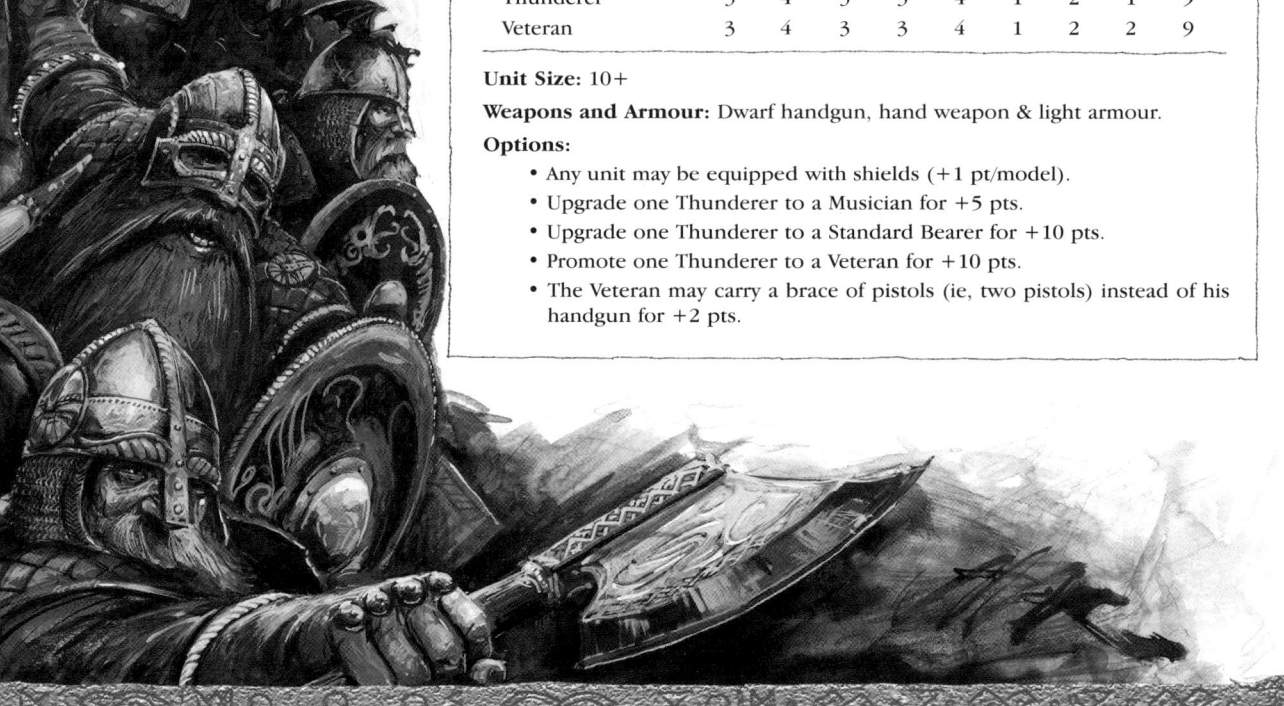

WARRIORS — Points/model: 7

	M	WS	BS	S	T	W	I	A	Ld
Warrior	3	4	3	3	4	1	2	1	9
Veteran	3	4	3	3	4	1	2	2	9

Unit Size: 10+.

Weapons and Armour: Hand weapon & light armour.

Options:
- Any unit may be equipped with heavy armour (+1 pt/model) and/or shields (+1 pt/model).
- Any unit may be equipped with Great Weapons (+2 pts/model).
- Upgrade one Warrior to a Musician for +5 pts.
- Upgrade one Warrior to a Standard Bearer for +10 pts.
- Promote one Warrior to a Veteran for +10 pts.

CROSSBOWMEN — Points/model: 12

	M	WS	BS	S	T	W	I	A	Ld
Crossbowman	3	4	3	3	4	1	2	1	9
Veteran	3	4	3	3	4	1	2	2	9

Unit Size: 10+

Weapons and Armour: Crossbow, hand weapon & light armour.

Options:
- Any unit may be equipped with shields (+1 pt/model).
- Upgrade one Crossbowman to a Musician for +5 pts.
- Upgrade one Crossbowman to a Standard Bearer for +10 pts.
- Promote one Crossbowman to a Veteran for +10 pts.

THUNDERERS — Points/model: 14

	M	WS	BS	S	T	W	I	A	Ld
Thunderer	3	4	3	3	4	1	2	1	9
Veteran	3	4	3	3	4	1	2	2	9

Unit Size: 10+

Weapons and Armour: Dwarf handgun, hand weapon & light armour.

Options:
- Any unit may be equipped with shields (+1 pt/model).
- Upgrade one Thunderer to a Musician for +5 pts.
- Upgrade one Thunderer to a Standard Bearer for +10 pts.
- Promote one Thunderer to a Veteran for +10 pts.
- The Veteran may carry a brace of pistols (ie, two pistols) instead of his handgun for +2 pts.

0–1 MINERS   Points/model: 12

	M	WS	BS	S	T	W	I	A	Ld
Miner	3	4	3	3	4	1	2	1	9
Prospector	3	4	3	3	4	1	2	2	9

Unit Size: 10-20

Weapons and Armour: Pick (Great Weapon), hand weapon & heavy armour.

Options:
- Upgrade one Miner to a Musician for +6 pts.
- Upgrade one Miner to a Standard Bearer for +12 pts.
- Promote one Miner to a Prospector for +12 pts.

Special Rules

Underground Advance (See page 11).

0–1 RANGERS   Points/model: 12

	M	WS	BS	S	T	W	I	A	Ld
Ranger	3	4	3	3	4	1	2	1	9
Veteran	3	4	3	3	4	1	2	2	9

Unit Size: 10-20.

Weapons and Armour: Great Weapon & light armour.

Options:
- The unit may be equipped with shields (+1 pt/model).
- The unit may be equipped with crossbows (+5 pts/model) or throwing axes (+3 pts/model).
- Upgrade one Ranger to a Musician for +6 pts.
- Upgrade one Ranger to a Standard Bearer for +12 pts.
- Promote one Ranger to a Veteran for +12 pts.

Special Rules

Scouts; Foresters (See page 10).

CORE UNITS

On this page are listed the troops who, whilst still being classed as Core Units, perform more specialised roles when Dwarfs go to war, the Rangers and the Miners.

Only one unit of **Miners** and one unit of **Rangers** may be fielded in an army.

SPECIAL UNITS

Special Units are extremely specialised troops which appear on the battlefield less often than Core Units.

There is a maximum number of Special Units that can be fielded, and this varies depending on the size of the army.

Hammerers are the personal bodyguard of a Dwarf King and are amongst the most skilled warriors in a Dwarf army.

Only one unit of Hammerers can be fielded in a Dwarf army.

All Dwarfs bear the Ancestral Grudge and are Relentless and Resolute (See page 6 for rules).

0-1 HAMMERERS — Points/model: 14

	M	WS	BS	S	T	W	I	A	Ld
Hammerer	3	5	3	4	4	1	2	1	9
Gate Keeper	3	5	3	4	4	1	2	2	9

Unit Size: 10+

Weapons and Armour: Great Weapon, hand weapon & heavy armour.

Options:
- Any unit may be equipped with shields (+1 pt/model).
- Upgrade one Hammerer to a Musician for +6 pts.
- Upgrade one Hammerer to a Standard Bearer for +12 pts.
- A Standard Bearer may carry a runic standard worth up to 50 pts.
- Promote one Hammerer to a Gate Keeper for +12 pts.

Special Rules
Bodyguard (See page 12).

LONGBEARDS — Points/model: 14

	M	WS	BS	S	T	W	I	A	Ld
Longbeard	3	5	3	4	4	1	2	1	9
Greatbeard	3	5	3	4	4	1	2	2	9

Unit Size: 10+

Weapons and Armour: Great Weapon, hand weapon, heavy armour & shield.

Options:
- Upgrade one Longbeard to a Musician for +6 pts.
- Upgrade one Longbeard to a Standard Bearer for +12 pts.
- A Standard Bearer may carry a runic standard worth up to 50 pts.
- Promote one Longbeard to a Greatbeard for +12 pts.

Special Rules
Immune to Panic (See page 13).

IRONBREAKERS — Points/model: 13

	M	WS	BS	S	T	W	I	A	Ld
Ironbreaker	3	5	3	4	4	1	2	1	9
Ironbeard	3	5	3	4	4	1	2	2	9

Unit Size: 10+

Weapons and Armour: Hand weapon, gromril armour & shield.

Options:
- Upgrade one Ironbreaker to a Musician for +6 pts.
- Upgrade one Ironbreaker to a Standard Bearer for +12 pts.
- A Standard Bearer may carry a runic standard worth up to 50 pts.
- Promote one Ironbreaker to an Ironbeard for +12 pts.

0-1 SLAYERS — Points/model: 11

	M	WS	BS	S	T	W	I	A	Ld
Troll Slayer	3	4	3	3	4	1	2	1	10
Giant Slayer	3	5	3	4	4	1	3	2	10

Unit Size: 10-30

Weapons and Armour: Slayers are extremely skilled with all manner of axes. Regardless of what weapons the model is carrying, Troll Slayers always count as being equipped with two hand weapons.

Options:
- Upgrade one Slayer to a Musician for +6 pts.
- Upgrade one Slayer to a Standard Bearer for +12 pts.
- Promote any number of Troll Slayers to Giant Slayers for +15 pts/model.

Special Rules
Slayer; Unbreakable (see page 7).

CANNON — Points/model: 100

	M	WS	BS	S	T	W	I	A	Ld
Cannon	–	–	–	–	7	3	–	–	–
Crew	3	4	3	3	4	1	2	1	9

Number of crew: 3

Crew's Weapons and Armour: Hand weapon & light armour.

Special Rules
See pages 122-124 of the Warhammer rulebook.

BOLT THROWER* — Points/model: 45

	M	WS	BS	S	T	W	I	A	Ld
Bolt Thrower	–	–	–	–	7	3	–	–	–
Crew	3	4	3	3	4	1	2	1	9

*Note that 1-2 Bolt Throwers count as only one Special Unit choice.

Number of crew: 3

Crew's Weapons and Armour: Hand weapon & light armour.

Special Rules
See pages 124-125 of the Warhammer rulebook.

STONE THROWER — Points/model: 85

	M	WS	BS	S	T	W	I	A	Ld
Stone Thrower	–	–	–	–	7	3	–	–	–
Crew	3	4	3	3	4	1	2	1	9

Number of crew: 3

Crew's Weapons and Armour: Hand weapon & light armour.

Special Rules
See pages 120-121 of the Warhammer rulebook.

SPECIAL UNITS

Although they usually prefer to fight alone, in times of war **Slayers** group together on the battlefield.

Only one unit of Slayers can be fielded in a Dwarf army.

The Dwarf army includes specialist artillery (**cannon**, **bolt throwers** and **stone throwers**) which they use to great effect.

Note that you may include either one or two Bolt Throwers as a single Special Unit choice.

RARE UNITS

Rare Units are the scarcest in the Dwarf army, comprising of the more recent war machines which have been invented by the Dwarf Engineers Guild.

These machines are viewed with sceptism by other Dwarfs who do not feel comfortable with a war engine unless it has proved itself in many battles over many centuries.

In times of great need a Dwarf Lord may open up his treasuries to hire mercenary units such as Long Drong's Slayers or Ludwig's Wondrous Grenadiers.

ORGAN GUN — Points/model: 125

	M	WS	BS	S	T	W	I	A	Ld
Organ Gun	–	–	–	–	7	3	–	–	–
Crew	3	4	3	3	4	1	2	1	9

Number of crew: 3

Crew's Weapons and Armour: Hand weapon & light armour.

Special Rules
See page 16.

FLAME CANNON — Points/model: 140

	M	WS	BS	S	T	W	I	A	Ld
Flame Cannon	–	–	–	–	7	3	–	–	–
Crew	3	4	3	3	4	1	2	1	9

Number of crew: 3

Crew's Weapons and Armour: Hand weapon & light armour.

Special Rules
See page 15.

GYROCOPTER — Points/model: 140

	M	WS	BS	S	T	W	I	A	Ld
Gyrocopter	–	–	–	–	5	3	–	–	–
Pilot	–	4	–	3	–	–	2	1	9

Pilot's Equipment: Hand weapon.

Armour Save: 4+

Special Rules
See page 17.

DOGS OF WAR — Points/model: variable

Dogs of War are mercenary units which you can hire to supplement your army.
You may opt to choose a unit of Dogs of War as a Dwarf Rare Unit.

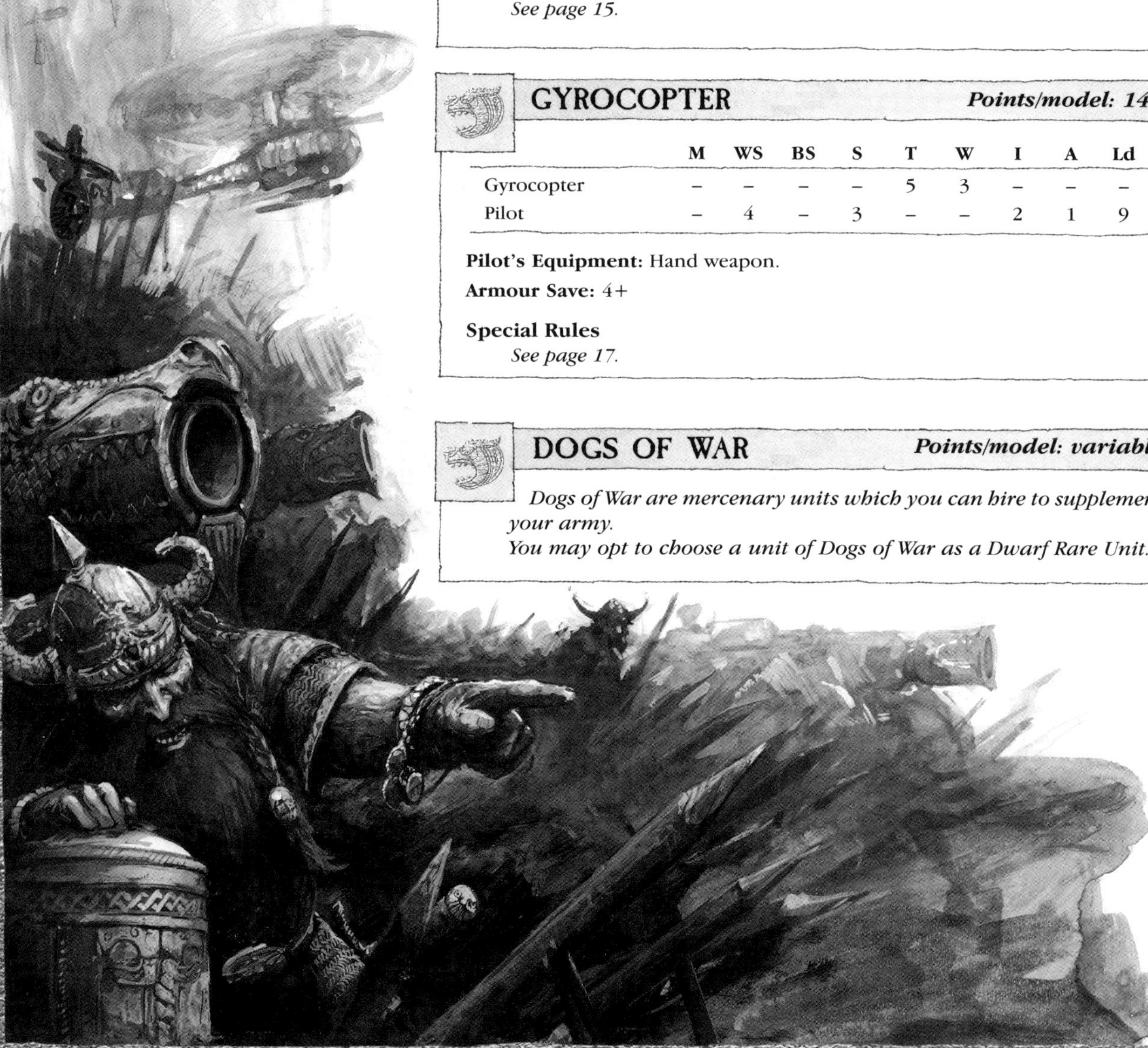

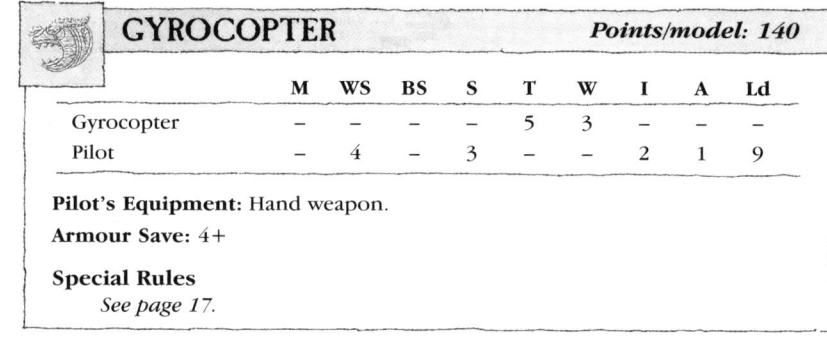

PAINTING THE DWARF ARMY

Two fully painted armies facing each other across a battlefield is an awesome sight. For many people it is the inspiration which sparks the desire to lead their own armies into battle. At first glance, painting a whole army may seem a little daunting. Don't worry though, you'd be surprised at how quickly your new army takes shape and how enjoyable the whole process actually is. Make no mistake, an army doesn't appear overnight, and it requires patience. However, the reward gained from owning and playing with a beautifully painted army makes all the effort more than worthwhile.

If you are a newcomer to Warhammer then don't worry about the quality of your painting. Many of the figures shown on the following pages are painted by the highly skilled 'Eavy Metal team. These talented guys and gals spend every day of the week painting figures and achieve standards that even those of us who have been painting for quite some time can only dream of matching. Whilst few of us will ever own a force painted to such extraordinarily high quality, this doesn't mean that we can't all aim to come close or even to better our standards with each new figure we paint. With time and patience, one day you may be the proud owner of a legendary Golden Demon award.

In this section of the book we will show you a variety of easy to learn techniques and tips with which to help you paint your regiments. In a short time you will have developed the skills necessary to invent your own methods and colour schemes to paint a truly unique army.

It is important to remember that there is no correct way to paint your army. The figures on the following pages are purely there for inspiration, and the more variety that you add to your own style, the better your enjoyment of the hobby will be for it. We have included several different methods and techniques. Try experimenting with them until you find the method that suits you best. If getting your army straight into battle is more important to you then choose a quick method. If you'd rather take your time painting an army that will make your friends drool with envy, then use some of the more detailed techniques to paint your models.

What we hope to achieve in the following pages, is to offer you a guide. The most important aspect to painting your army is that you have fun. Relax and enjoy yourself and before you know it you'll find that very soon you might be starting on your second or third army!

PAINTING DWARFS

Dwarfs are famed for their finely-crafted armour and long beards, so you're going to be painting lots of models covered in metal and hair! Once you've mastered these simple techniques you should finish your Dwarf regiments in no time.

As you begin to paint your army you will develop ideas as to what colour schemes your army will adopt. We have chosen to introduce a neutral Dark Ages tone into our units rather than bright vivid hues. These colours capture the character of the Dwarfs but by no means think that this will result in a drab, bland army. Use of simple contrasting colours, even within a limited palette, will make your regiments stand out on the tabletop.

With any army that requires a great deal of armour and weaponry to be painted, we recommend that you undercoat your figures Chaos Black. This produces a better result for painting armour.

Drybrushing is a useful technique for painting the textured surface of both armour and beards. Dip your brush into your chosen colour and then wipe away most of the paint onto a paper towel. By dragging your brush lightly across the model a small quantity of paint will adhere to the surface of the miniature, picking out the texture. Drybrushing can be combined with a coat of ink to add extra shading. Dwarfs usually have a relatively small area of cloth showing but what colour you paint this is important as you may wish to link it in with your overall army colour scheme.

There are lots of ways to paint metal, here are two. 1. Chainmail with a Black Ink wash. 2. Chainmail drybrushed over a black undercoat.

Here is a simple stage by stage for painting a Dwarf warrior. Stage 1. Start by painting all the base colours first. We begin by drybrushing the armour and weapons Boltgun Metal. The beard has been painted Snakebite Leather and as we have decided on a green colour scheme for our army the trim around the armour has been painted Dark Angels Green. The helmet has been painted with Tinbitz. The flesh has been painted with Dwarf Flesh. Once you've got to this point you can stop if you want to and start gaming. Simply paint the base a suitable colour such as Goblin Green. Later on you can add extra details and highlights to the model.

Stage 2. The base colours are dark enough not to need shading. Instead, a layer of highlights is added to the figure. The armour is highlighted with a light drybrush of Mithril Silver. The beard has been drybrushed with Bubonic Brown. A mix of Dark Angels Green and Camo Green was used for the trim and Dwarf Bronze has been used to highlight the helmet. The flesh has been highlighted with a touch of Elf Flesh.

Stage 3. Bleached Bone is drybrushed on the tips of the moustache and beard. The trim has been highlighted with a fine layer of Camo green. A good base will dramatically improve the overall appearance of a figure. In this case the base is painted Goblin Green and flock is glued on with PVA once the paint has dried. There are a number of ways you can base your figures, including using sand instead of flock but whichever method you select you will find that using a common technique to base your army with will make them look much more cohesive.

Here are some examples of different techniques for painting beards. 1. Flat colour of Snakebite Leather. 2. Snakebite Leather with Brown Ink Wash. 3. Snakebite Leather highlighted with Bubonic Brown. 4. Snakebite Leather with Brown Ink Wash and Snakebite Leather highlights followed by Bubonic Brown highlights painted on.

Here are some ideas for different colours of beards. 1. Sunburst Yellow. 2. Fiery Orange. 3. Chaos Black. 4. Vermin Brown. Also try using Fortress Grey, Leprous Brown, Shadow Grey and Scorched Brown.

The 'Eavy Metal team painted warriors in a variety of colour schemes before finally deciding on the green warriors of Karak-Hirn. Shown here are other colour variants which they found worked well together. You may wish to use one of these schemes or alternatively they may inspire you to create your own.

PAINTING THE DWARF ARMY

Standards are used to differentiate between the units within your army. This is of great practical importance when fighting battles as you can quickly identify where units are on the table. When deciding how to paint your standards, consideration should be given to how the colours you choose can be used to tie the unit together. By using similar icons and colour schemes on the standard as the models have on their shields and clothes, your figures will look like they belong to that regiment and no other.

Paul Sawyer combined a Warmaster Anvil of Doom model and a Dark Elf standard to make his unique Standard Bearer.

Dwarfs are proud of their beards and it's one of the most prominent parts of the figure. Use the beard to make each Dwarf in a unit look like an individual. To do this you may decide to paint each Dwarf with a different coloured beard. Rather than pick lots of different colours you can choose one colour and make it lighter or darker by adding white or black. Changing a colour's tone like this is a useful way to add variety in a Dwarf army without using too many colours.

As you paint more Dwarfs to make complete regiments you will find, as you'll see here and over the next few pages, that shields and standards are the simplest way to unify all of the models within a particular unit. The shield is one of the prominent features of many Dwarf figures and will be one of the areas that the eye is drawn to first. Therefore it is well worth considering a colour scheme for your shields and how this scheme will relate to your army when it is finished.

A simple and effective method is to use the different icons on the shields to distinguish between each unit. Alternatively you may decide to use the same icon throughout your army and use variations on colour or pattern to differentiate between each unit. You may even decide to paint the shield and leave off the icon altogether. You can also use transfers, or paint on a design if you are feeling particularly artistic. By painting the cloth on your figure with the same colour scheme that you have used on the shields the unit will look far more cohesive.

THE WARRIORS OF KARAK-HIRN

The shields have a Dark Angels Green background, whilst the icons have been painted Shining Gold. On one we have painted a tankard.

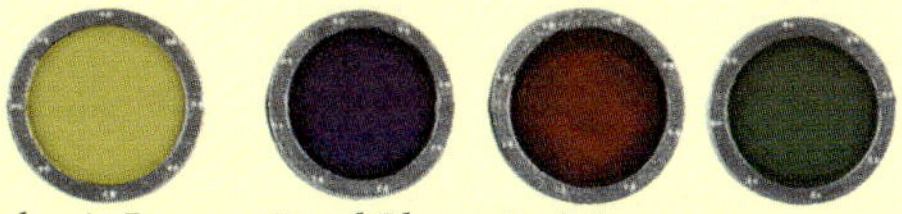

Bubonic Brown   **Regal Blue**   **Red Gore**   50/50 mix of Snot Green & Dark Angels Green

The four shields above show some examples of Dark Age colours that capture the character of the Dwarfs. These colours combine well with the Dwarfs' bright armour and beards, to achieve a striking effect.

THRONG OF KARAK NORN

The warriors of Karak Norn use a red and blue colour scheme with white as a contrast colour.

The icons can either be painted metallic or in a variety of colours to contrast against the shield's background colour.

35

PAINTING THE DWARF ARMY

DWARF REGIMENTS

When painting a Dwarf army, or in fact any army, you may want to consider it in terms of whole regiments rather than individual figures. The colour schemes you use for your regiments will dictate the overall look of your army.

The bulk of a Dwarf army consists of solid blocks of foot troops. It is therefore important to decide on a colour scheme for your regiments in advance as this will affect how your army looks. There are a number of different ways to paint regiments. You may decide to paint your army with one overall colour scheme or you may choose to paint each regiment a different colour to distinguish between them. Either way it is important that you stick with this theme as you continue to paint all of the models in that regiment.

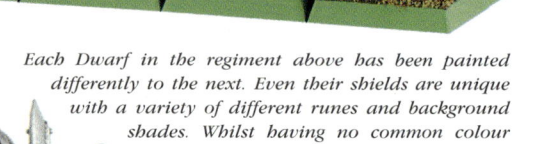

Each Dwarf in the regiment above has been painted differently to the next. Even their shields are unique with a variety of different runes and background shades. Whilst having no common colour scheme their bases are consistent, they have a common colour tone and look as though they are warriors who have hastily gathered together to defend their hold.

An alternative approach to painting each model as an individual is to choose a common theme for the army. The Karak-Hirn army has been painted with a green theme to it. Each warriors' shield in the unit has the same gold icon on a green background, complemented by green trim on their armour. This is because the stronghold has a particular affiliation with those colours. A subtle variation in tones has been used to paint the clothing and the beards are a variety of colours, adding an individual feel to the warriors. Whatever the reason behind your scheme, finding a theme with which to paint your regiments can be inspirational and adds an extra dimension to the overall effect. Martin Footitt and the 'Eavy Metal team used Dark Angels Green on the armour trim and shield background. The armour and weapons were painted in Chainmail and highlighted with Mithril Silver. Finally the icons were painted with Shining Gold and given a wash of Chestnut Ink.

While our Karak-Hirn army is themed with the use of green in different places, we wanted our Karak Norn army to have more of a definite uniform. In this case we chose a mix of blue and red with white as a contrast colour, used in a rigid scheme within each regiment. The 'Eavy Metal team used Regal Blue to paint the cloth, with Enchanted Blue highlights. The weapons were painted with Boltgun Metal and highlighted with Mithril Silver. Shining Gold was used for each standard, washed with Chestnut Ink. Their striking red trim is a mixture of Red Gore and Blood Red. The shield icon is the same throughout the entire army but the background varies from unit to unit, in this case the shield is red and white to match the unit's standard.

36

PAINTING THE DWARF ARMY

ASSEMBLING REGIMENTS

Before you plunge into painting your regiments it is worthwhile giving a little thought to how the models fit together. Models which 'rank up' will look a lot better once they are on the battlefield.

It is a good idea to assemble your regiments before you begin to paint them. Whilst models can look great in a variety of poses it defeats the purpose of making spectacular looking regiments if you simply can't rank them up into units. A little bit of forethought can save you hours of work later. Try assembling your models in ranks first. Stand the models next to each other as you glue them together to make sure they rank up. Models in the front rank or those at the sides can be assembled in more dynamic poses whilst the models in the centre of the unit should stand together neatly. You may find it useful to glue some of your models onto the long plastic regiment bases. This will save you an enormous amount of time when you come to place your models on the battlefield.

The weapons and shields of this Karak-Hirn regiment have been positioned so they don't interfere with the model next to them, allowing the bases to square up neatly.

Some of these Dwarfs have been glued onto regimental bases. This makes it far easier to set up your units. The figures in the rear rank have been put on individual bases which allows individual casualties to be removed.

GAV THORPE'S KARAK AZUL THRONG

The blue colour scheme Gav has used for his Dwarf warriors has also been carried over onto his war machines. He either uses white, purple or red as contrasting colours on gloves, weapon hafts and other details. The wholly metallic shields of the warriors also give them a distinctive look, painted with a drybrush of Chainmail over a black undercoat. The Slayers and Miners are painted to contrast with the rest of the army, making these special units stand out.

37

PAINTING THE DWARF ARMY

Crossbows

There are some easy solutions to identifying individual units without shields. The Crossbow unit from Karak-Hirn shown here are identified by the green trim of their armour and brown tunics. Another option is to paint their weapons in your chosen colour.

Many of the figures have unique features such as tankards and pipes. Although these may be hidden somewhat by the shield it is still worthwhile to place such models in the front rank of your army so they can be seen.

This Crossbow regiment uses the same shield icon and red, blue and white colours to identify itself as part of the Karak Norn army. Every shield in the army uses the same icon, but with different backgrounds to distinguish between regiments. The entire army has adopted a red and blue colour scheme on its clothing, which is applied in a variety of styles to each regiment to characterise them as part of the same force.

Much like the Crossbow regiment at the top, these Handgunners have been painted using the same tones of brown and all have the same green trim to identify them as part of the Karak-Hirn army.

They have been given an individual feel through painting their beards and gloves in a variety of different colours.

These Thunderers' handguns have had the details highlighted with Shining Gold.

Karak Norn Crossbows

38

PAINTING THE DWARF ARMY

Longbeards

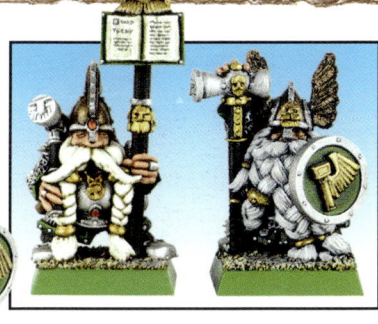

Paul Sawyer's Longbeards

Much of a Longbeard model is covered up by his extraordinary long beard. We have used a variety of different basecoats such as Codex Grey and Snakebite Leather on these models. They have then been highlighted to white to give the unit a unified feel, yet with subtle variation. The rings on their beards have been painted with Shining Gold to reflect the age and status of this venerable regiment.

Ironbreakers wear thick suits of armour to protect them in battle. As a result the model is predominantly painted in metallic colours. To break up the silver armour we have painted the runes on their armour Shining Gold. The shield's green background identifies them as part of the Karak-Hirn army. Some variety has been added to the unit by painting the beards in different colours.

Ironbreakers

Bodyguards to the King, the Hammerers unit are distinguished by gold breatplates and a large amount of gold trim. The models each have an individual feel even though they are in similar poses as there is a wide variation in the colour of their beards. They still have green cloth on them, once again distinguishing them as part of the Karak-Hirn army. More advanced techniques such as painting a gemstone on the hammer can really make a figure stand out.

A unit of Hammerers form the King's own bodyguard. As such their armour is painted gold to reflect their high status.

PAINTING THE DWARF ARMY

TROLLSLAYERS

Most Dwarf armies will field a unit of Trollslayers. These self exiled Dwarfs are unique amongst the Dwarf units in that they don't wear armour and dye their beards a bright orange colour. Because of this a different approach is needed when painting a regiment of these fearless warriors.

The most striking feature of a Trollslayer is the mass of thick, fiery orange hair. Here we have undercoated the figure Skull White and then painted a base coat of Blazing Orange followed by a drybrush of Fiery Orange on top as a highlight. As they don't wear armour there is a far greater area of skin to paint. In this example we've used a basecoat of Dark Flesh and painted over this with Dwarf Flesh. A mix of Dwarf Flesh and Bleached Bone then provides the final highlight colour. We've added blue tattoos to the figures to give them a wild, frightening appearance. Although Trollslayers are exiles and have no clan allegiance, we chose to paint some of their trousers green as part of the Karak-Hirn army colour scheme.

Trollslayers

Another way to paint Dwarf skin is to start with a coat of Dwarf Flesh and then shade it with Flesh Ink or even watered down Red Ink. Try painting the Trollslayer's beard Golden Yellow and shade it with Orange or Red Ink, or perhaps start with Blood Red as a base colour and then drybrush with Fiery Orange and Bad Moon Yellow. You might like to vary the different shades of orange beard within the unit.

PAUL ROWLEY'S DWARFS

Paul Rowley took his Dwarf army to the 1997 Grand Tournament where it won the Best Army award. As you can see he has used a striking orange and green colour scheme. "Without it I don't think I'd have painted them as quickly as I did. I didn't know exactly how every model would look but I did know exactly what colours I wanted to use and could think about where to put those colours on each model or unit." Using the same colour scheme throughout the entire army has distinct advantages. Models become easier to paint because repeating the same colours makes you get used to painting models and the more you do the better the results will be. Simple ideas such as painting all the hammer shafts red can also make your units stand out.

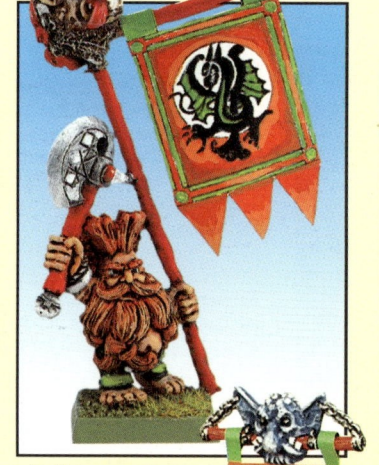

Hammerer

Trollslayer with converted standard

Left: Trollslayers. Above: Hammerers.

PAINTING THE DWARF ARMY

BUGMAN'S RANGERS

Famed more for his strong ale than his exploits on the battlefield, Josef Bugman is a legend amongst the Dwarf world. With the destruction of his brewery his Rangers now scour the mountains seeking revenge on Goblin and Orcs alike.

The famous Bugman's brewery was located near to Karak Norn and we wanted the unit of Rangers in the army to represent the legendary Bugman's Rangers themselves. To tie them in to the rest of the Karak Norn army, they have a split colour scheme of red and blue, which is carried through to their banner and shields. For units which you want to make into a focal point of your army it is worthwhile spending a bit more time on each model when highlighting and shading.

Above: These rangers from our Karak-Hirn army have been painted in browns and greens. The colour of the horns on their helmets was created with a base colour of Bubonic Brown which was then highlighted with Bleached Bone towards the tips.

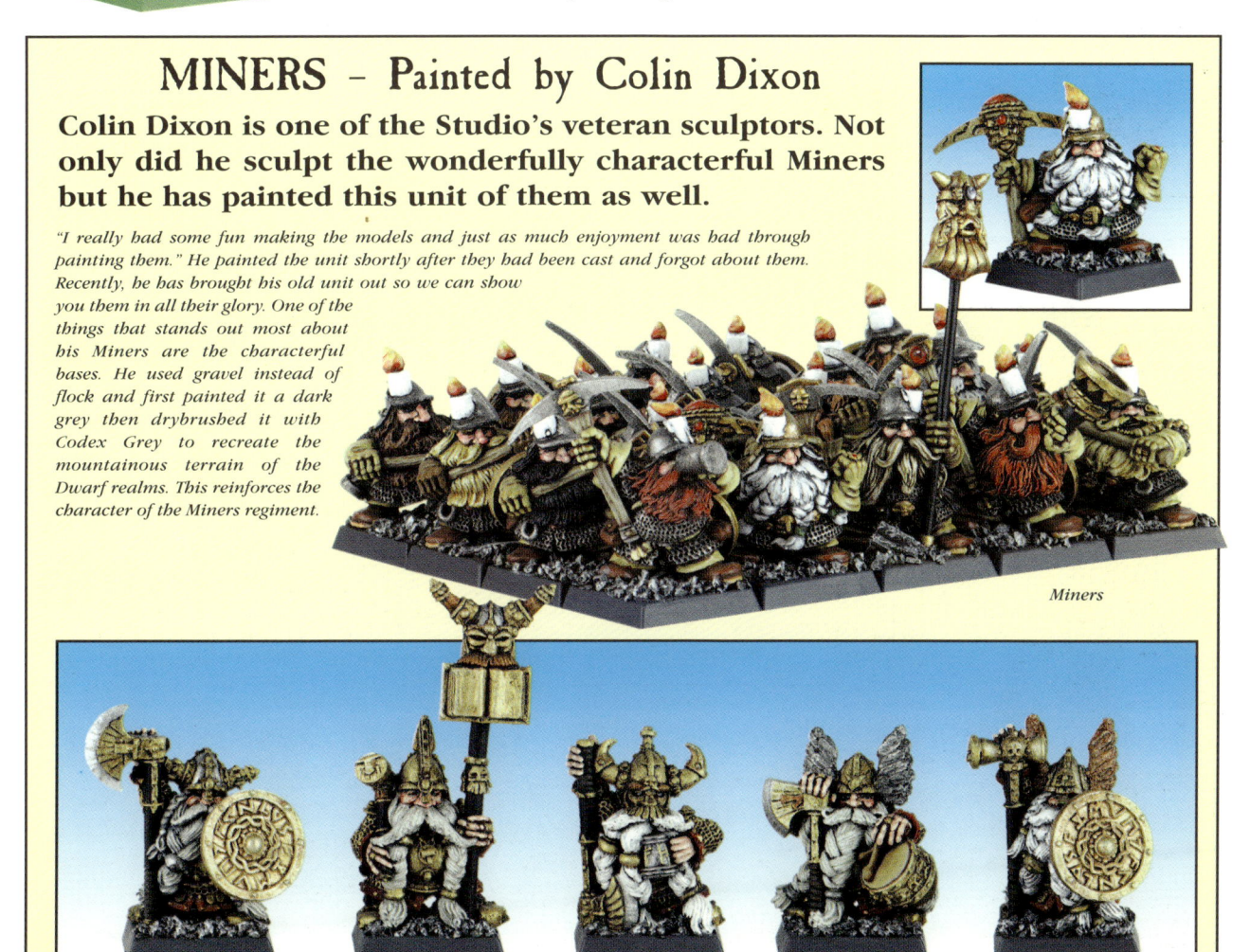

Bugman's Rangers

MINERS – Painted by Colin Dixon

Colin Dixon is one of the Studio's veteran sculptors. Not only did he sculpt the wonderfully characterful Miners but he has painted this unit of them as well.

"I really had some fun making the models and just as much enjoyment was had through painting them." He painted the unit shortly after they had been cast and forgot about them. Recently, he has brought his old unit out so we can show you them in all their glory. One of the things that stands out most about his Miners are the characterful bases. He used gravel instead of flock and first painted it a dark grey then drybrushed it with Codex Grey to recreate the mountainous terrain of the Dwarf realms. This reinforces the character of the Miners regiment.

Miners

Colin's Longbeards

41

PAINTING THE DWARF ARMY

WAR ENGINES

The Dwarf army contains a wide variety of powerful machines of destruction. These machines stand out on the battlefield and are amongst the largest models in the entire army.

When assembling the base section of a Gyrocopter it is useful to glue the clear plastic base onto the larger 40mm square base. This makes it far easier to use when fighting in close combat.

Flame cannon

War machines such as Flame cannons are made of metal and wood. The metal can be painted using the same techniques that apply for armour. The wooden sections can be painted Scorched Brown and highlighted with Bestial Brown, or another suitable combination of wood-like colours. You may wish to paint the wooden parts with the colour theme of your army. Either way the crew can be painted to fit in with the rest of your units and you may want to distinguish between separate crews for each war machine in your army by giving them a unique uniform. The Flame Cannon above has been painted green in keeping with the rest of the Karak-Hirn army, whilst the Bolt Thrower below has the feathers on its bolts painted red to fit the red and blue colour scheme of the Karak Norn army.

Dwarf Bolt Thrower

Dwarf Engineer from Karak-Hirn

Dwarf artillery: Flame Cannon, Bolt Thrower and Stone Thrower.

PAINTING THE DWARF ARMY

KAZAD BOLG EXPEDITIONARY FORCE by Paul Sawyer

In the spare time that 'Fat Bloke' manages to find, when not busy putting together the next issue of White Dwarf, he has painted a Dwarf army that really stands out on the battlefield.

Dwarf Miner

Dwarf Cannon

Longbeards

Gyrocopter

The army is themed around the Dwarfs of Kazad Bolg. Paul has opted for a bright colour scheme of a simple yellow and black combination which he has used throughout the entire force. He has a considerable amount of firepower in the army and the scheme has been adopted on every war machine. Even his Trollslayers have half of their faces painted black.

PAINTING THE DWARF ARMY

ANVIL OF DOOM

The Anvil of Doom is an ancient and valuable heirloom. When fielded in battle it is a great centrepiece for your army. This magnificent model is a marvellous opportunity to show off your painting skills.

We have continued to use the colour scheme of Karak-Hirn by painting the shields green. Take your time to pick out some of the finer details and make full use of the techniques you have acquired through painting the rest of your army. The more patience you display when painting this model, the greater your reward will be.

44

PAINTING THE DWARF ARMY

The Lord of Kazak-Hirn leads his bodyguard to battle.

Dwarf Miners

A large force of Dwarfs amass to defend Bugman's Brewery from the bloodthirsty ambitions of an approaching Chaos Horde.

THE DWARF ARMY OF KARAK-HIRN

PAINTING THE DWARF ARMY

The Karak-Hirn army prepares to defend their hold from the onslaught of an Orc horde. As you can see, the green colour scheme that have the 'Eavy Metal team has chosen unifies the whole army. By sticking to a few basic colours the final result is very effective. With subtle variations in details such as banners, each unit can develop its own unique appearance whilst still fitting in with the overall army colour scheme. As you can see, the reward from some careful planning before you start painting your army can be very impressive.

MAKING TERRAIN

The perfect addition to a fully painted Dwarf army is to create some Dwarf themed terrain. It will not only add to the overall look of your army but will liven up your battles too. Such terrain is both fun to make and will give you a marvellous sense of achievement.

1) To make a rocky hill for your Dwarf terrain start with a piece of tree bark (bought from a pet store), a piece of polystyrene and hardboard cut into a rough shape. You can use thick cardboard instead of the hardboard if you like. Cut the polystyrene into a rough mound shape with a hot wire cutter (available from Mail Order). Allow a little room down one edge of the hill for the bark to form the rock face. 2) Glue the polystyrene to the base with PVA glue. Either break the bark into small chunks and glue it into place or cut it into shape with a saw. Fill any large gaps with modelling putty and paint the whole model with sand mixed with PVA or, if you prefer, textured paint. Once dry, glue on some large stones and fill any small gaps with gravel or sand. Spray the hill black and drybrush the rocks Shadow Grey, Codex Grey and then Skull White. 3) Finally, paint the top of the hill green then paint with PVA glue and sprinkle flock over the top to give the appearance of grass. For more about making terrain check out White Dwarf or the Hobby Projects page at our web site (www.games-workshop.com).

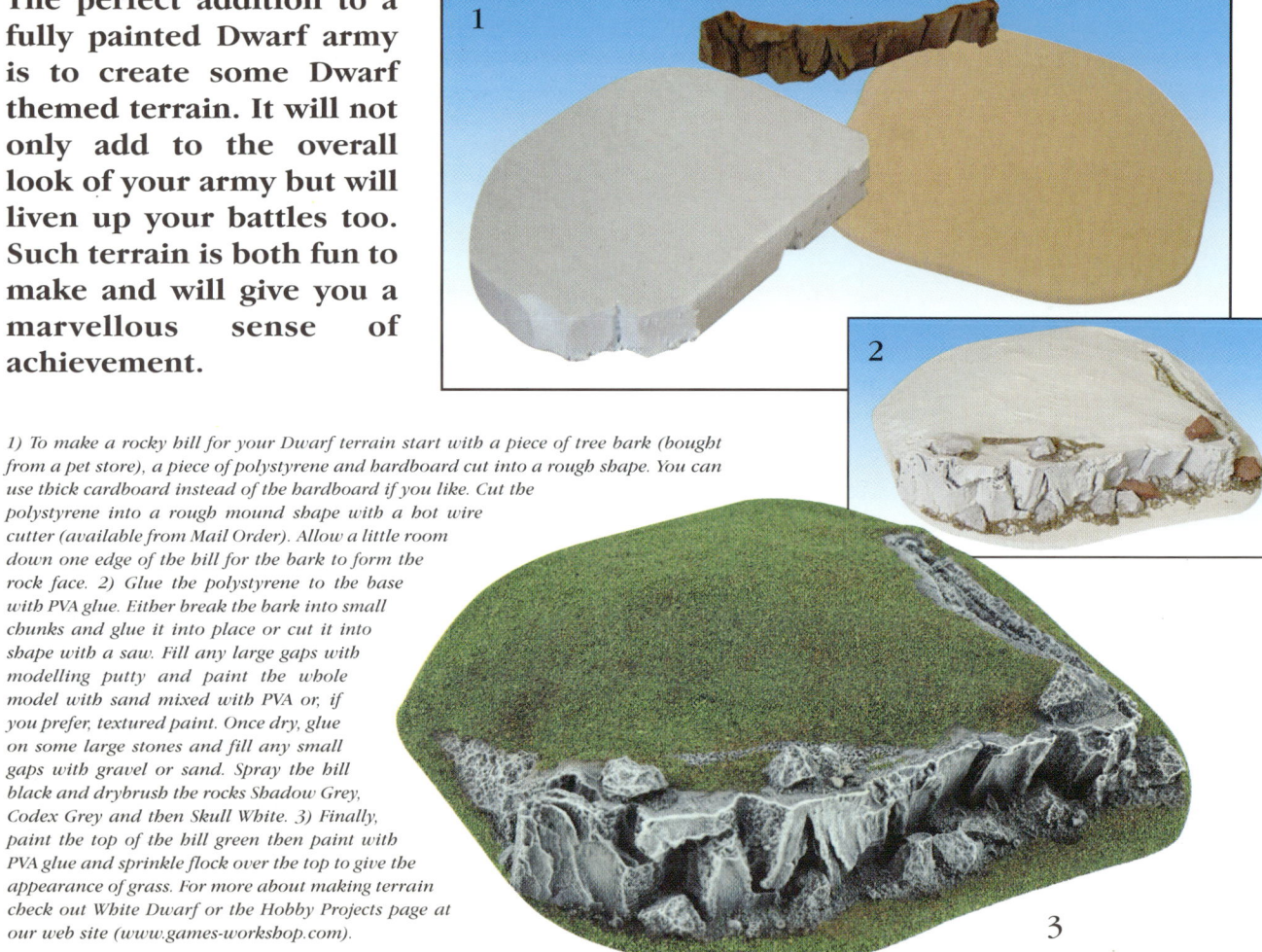

This feature is a Citadel Terrain piece. It has been painted and the base flocked to blend into the table top. The cliff face is made from chunks of tree bark which you can buy from pet stores. The surface is painted with textured paint to give it a rocky texture.

DWARFS OF LEGEND

The history of the Dwarfs is one of battle. They have been betrayed by their former allies and their homes have been overrun by countless monsters from the depths. But in all this time the Dwarfs have not given up hope. They are stubborn to a fault in their unwillingness to contemplate surrender, and even the loss of one of their ancestral Holds is seen as only a temporary setback. Their Golden Age will come again, or so they believe. However, there are some of their number who stand out as exceptional even amongst this race of valiant warriors, and as the Dwarfs never forget either a favour or a slight we can recount a few of those tales here.

This page lists the most famous of these mighty heroes. Feel free to expand on what's here; work out game statistics and so on for these characters if you want to include them in your games. The following pages include full details for two characters: Thorek Ironbrow and King Alrik of Karak-Hirn. You may use either of these in your games of Warhammer by paying the points as normal.

You do not need to agree with your opponent about using either Thorek or Alrik as they are balanced for normal games. However, if you wish to use any new characters of your own devising, or want to use expanded versions of the ones on this page, then you must agree with your opponent before the battle.

UNGRIM IRONFIST, THE SLAYER KING OF KARAK KADRIN

The meaning of the unfortunate Ungrim's name, 'oathbound', tells his story well for he is bound by two oaths that he cannot reconcile. The first is his loyalty to the people he rules, the second is his inherited Slayer oath to seek a noble death – something he cannot honourably do whilst his people still need him!

GOTREK GURNISSON & FELIX JAEGAR

Just as in the sagas of old, this mismatched pair of adventurers seem doomed to wander the world until the fate the gods have decreed for them is at hand. Legend has it that the man, Felix, a minor poet and general ne'er-do-well, fell in with the Slayer Gotrek during an epic drinking binge. It is said that Felix made a vow to enshrine Gotrek's quest for a noble death in a poem, and that he would stay with him until his doom came to pass. It is an oath he has learned to consider a trifle hasty as it has led him into the darkest and most lethal corners of the Old World and pitted them against the most heinous of foes. Gotrek, however, seems all but unkillable and, as long as he breathes, Felix cannot find it in his honour to break his oath. Who knows which battlefields they will fight on next, or which monstrosity will finally be Gotrek's doom?

HIGH KING THORGRIM GRUDGEBEARER

With the blood of Grungni himself running in his royal veins, it is hardly surprising that Thorgim is deeply concerned with the fate of his race. It is this concern that makes the Dammaz Kron, the Great Book of Grudges of the Dwarfs, his constant companion. Whether it is resting beneath his pillow at night or accompanying him to one of his many battles atop the Throne of Power, Dammaz Kron is never far from his side. Thorgim rules from the heights of Karaz-a-Karak and ventures forth frequently to avenge one or other of the many wrongs he has studied in Dammaz Kron. Even though the Dwarfs are reluctant to go to war and risk the lives of their diminishing number of warriors, the cause of vengeance is considered so just that they rally to Thorgrim with eagerness and follow him wherever he leads.

JOSEF BUGMAN

The most famed Dwarf Master Brewer of all time, his Bugman's XXXXXX is responsible for many a royal hangover. Since the tranquility of his peaceful brewery was smashed by Goblin raiders who destroyed the vats and killed or enslaved his workers, Bugman has sworn revenge and now fights greenskins wherever he can. His small band of Rangers are seldom noticed as they roam the Badlands in search of Goblins to slaughter and prisoners to rescue, but every now and again they will turn up at a Dwarf camp to offer their aid as the army readies for battle.

BURLOK DAMMINSON, ENGINEER GUILDMASTER

Burlok has been an engineer for centuries, and although something of a rebel in his youth, the loss of his arm in an accident and a furious reprimand from his father showed Burlok the error of his ways. Now he is a staunch traditionalist and resists any thought of innovation in the Dwarf Engineers' Guild. His missing arm has been replaced by a mechanical contrivance of his own devising, and over the many years since the accident he has improved it so that it now works even better than his natural arm.

THOREK IRONBROW, DWARF RUNELORD, MASTER OF THE WEAPON SHOPS OF KARAK AZUL

"Now you young 'uns might be thinking that nowt's as good as it used to be," grumbled Durgrim Redmane, eyeing the gathered beardlings. "Well there's summat in that, but it's not all bad. Take this here tavern," he continued, including the whole of the smoky room with a wave of his hand. "Couple of hundred years ago this was all rock." His drunken audience admired the bar anew with bleary eyes.

"And that's not all. There are even a few folk, like myself, who try to follow the old ways. Not many, but enough to give you young 'uns all hope. Take old Ironbrow, f'rinstance. You've all heard of him, haven't you?" Durgrim glanced over the rim of his ale mug at the attentive Dwarfs, but didn't bother waiting for a reply. "Thorek's a Dwarf of the old times. Karak Azgal's where he lives and where he's master of the armouries. Lucky lot to have him too. He's got one of them Anvils of Doom that were made by Kurgaz and he knows more of its secrets than most of those that have 'em.

He's also not afraid to use the power in it, not like some so-called Runelords I could mention. Anyway, like I was saying, he's a proper old fashioned Dwarf with little time for them modern ideas on how to forge weapons and armour. Nor does he care what runes are fashionable this century or that. If it was good enough for our ancestors in the War of Vengeance, it's good enough for Thorek Ironbrow. I've heard him say as much himself, and I felt right proud to hear it.

Now I can see that some of you are thinking 'What about progress?' Well, that's all nonsense. Anyone can tell you that's just muddle-headed Elf thinking. After all, we're doing worse not better, and what we really need is a return to the good old days, not some new-fangled replacement for things that weren't broke. Thorek Ironbrow is a worthy role model for any of you that fancy yourselves as Runesmiths. You could do a lot worse than try to impress him with your skill and understanding of the old ways, though it'll be right hard. He demands the highest standards and expects nothing less than your total commitment. Can't afford to mess with the power of an Anvil of Doom if you're all half-hearted." Durgrim paused, a far away look in his eyes.

"When they were made, all the Anvils could use the rune they're named for, but now I reckon it's just Thorek's that can do that. Mainly that's down to old Ironbrow himself. He knows more about the runes than any other Dwarf alive, and that's just 'cos he's spent his whole life reading the ancient texts and talking with the oldest and wisest Runelords." Durgrim eyed his audience carefully. "And paying attention to his elders."

THOREK IRONBROW

	M	WS	BS	S	T	W	I	A	Ld
Thorek	3	6	4	4	5	3	3	2	10
Kraggi	3	4	3	3	4	1	2	1	9

Thorek is the Master Runelord of Karak Azul and, some say, the greatest Runelord alive. He can be taken as a Lord choice in a Dwarf army, but will also take up one of your Hero choices as well. He must be fielded exactly as presented, and no extra equipment or rune items can be bought for him. The cost of his rune items, Anvil of Doom, Kraggi and two Anvil Guards is included in his total cost.

Points: 505. Note that while Thorek still lives, no Victory points are scored – this is different to the normal Anvil of Doom rules.

Weapons: The rune-hammer Klad Brakak.

Armour: Thorek's rune-armour.

RUNE ITEMS

Klad Brakak: Thorek's anvil-headed hammer is a formidable weapon of war as well as a useful tool. In his position as Master of the Weapon Smiths of Karak Azul he has access to a vast amount of ancient rune lore. From his researches and experiments, he has designed a new rune which he has struck onto his hammer. This rune is unique to Thorek's hammer, Klad Brakak, as he only made it a couple of centuries ago and wants to give it a fair trial before using it again.

In battle it is easy to find Thorek as his hammer shatters armour when it strikes, making a sound like thunder. No armour saves are allowed against Klad Brakak and if the target fails its Ward save (or does not have one) then any armour they were wearing and shield they were carrying are destroyed. This includes magical armour and shields.

In addition, Klad Brakak bears the Rune of Fury which gives Thorek +1 Attack (see page 20).

Thorek's rune-armour: This is inscribed with the Master Rune of Gromril (see page 21).

ANVIL OF DOOM

Thorek always brings his Anvil of Doom with him to battle. This works exactly as described on pages 8 & 9 with the additions noted below.

Assistant at the forge: Kraggi, the best of Thorek's assistants, accompanies him to battle and helps him by preparing some of the runes. Most of the time this is a big help and speeds things up, but occasionally his lack of experience (he's hardly been smithing a century) lets him down and he makes a mistake. Kraggi is treated as a unit Champion and fights with his forge tongs (counts as a hand weapon) and wears an apron to protect him from the intense heat (light armour).

While Kraggi is alive Thorek gains one extra dice per turn to cast runes with. However, it's important to keep track of which one this is (by using a different coloured dice, for example) because if this extra dice rolls a 1 Kraggi has done something wrong and the rune is miscast.

RUNE OF DOOM   12+ to cast

When Kurgaz forged the Anvils of Doom many centuries ago the most potent rune they had beaten onto them was the Rune of Doom, after which they were named. However, this rune is so difficult and dangerous to use that its secret has almost been lost. Some have not ever dared to use it or have never seen a threat they deemed sufficient to warrant its power. Others have tried and failed to contain and focus its might and their anvils have been torn apart by the uncontrolled energies. Today, the only remaining Runelord who has the skill and courage to attempt it is Thorek Ironbrow.

When this rune is struck, the air grows chill and the skies turn dark. Ghostly forms of ancient warriors appear amidst the Dwarfs on the battlefield, bolstering their ranks and their courage. These are not ghosts as such, but a manifestation of the Dwarfs' own grim and doom-laden nature. Their anger at the loss of their mighty civilisation and the desecration of their Holds fills them with a righteous fury that is terrible to behold, and their normally grim faces are set with an expression of black vengeance.

All the Dwarfs in the army cause *fear*.

Once cast, the effects of the Rune of Doom last until it is dispelled, until Thorek chooses to end it (which he can do at any time), uses another rune, or is slain.

However, if you miscast when rolling to cast the Rune of Doom then disaster has struck. The power of the rune tears the Anvil asunder. Thorek, Kraggi and any surviving Anvil Guards each take a single Strength 7 hit from the blast. The Anvil is destroyed and the survivors form a skirmishing unit.

Note that as you've been reminded of the doom of your race and that your Golden Age has long passed you should feel free to grumble about it (and don't forget to mention that it's the Elves' fault). This has no game effect, but is entirely in character and may make you feel better.

DWARF KING ALRIK RANULFSSON OF KARAK-HIRN

"Now if anyone could help soothe the parched throat of an old warrior I could continue. When I was a young 'un there was never any need for a battle-scarred veteran to ask for a drink as his cup was always full. Nor was... oh, thank you." Durgrim drained the newly-filled flagon in a single long draught, wiping the foam from his moustache with the back of his hand as he banged the mug on the table to be filled again.

"Now where was I? Oh yes. The few noble Dwarfs left that keep the old ways. Thorek I've told you about, but there's also King Alrik Ranulfsson of Karak-Hirn.

Even though he has to deal with all the lesser races who come to trade with him, King Alrik has stayed true to the old ways. The army of Karak-Hirn is a sight to make your heart glad, with ranks of Clansmen and Ironbreakers backed up by loyal Dwarfs with crossbows. Just like it was in the old days. None of your modern rubbish like flame cannons and Gyrocopters littering the place and stinking up the clean mountain air with their fumes. Don't know what those engineers were thinking. anyhow.

Karak-Hirn is one of the younger holds, founded after the Great Quakes. It was a tragic time and what were needed were great leaders. The founder of Karak-Hirn, Alrik's great-great-great-grandfather, was one such Dwarf. Kurgaz was probably the tallest and strongest of our kind ever to smite an Elf. He stood head and shoulders above his followers and could lift an entire ore wagon single-handed. As he fled the disasters of those dark times with his army of followers, he happened upon the mountain which would be his new home: Karak-Hirn, the Hornhold. Kurgaz was camped with his kinsmen above ground in a small valley, an unusual and troubling practice but necessary when the trembling earth is twisting even the finest Dwarf-wrought tunnels. As dusk drew in, the deep blare of a Dwarf warhorn sounded across the valley. Thinking his kind were in danger, Kurgaz rallied his bodyguard about him and set off towards the sound. They climbed for hours, feeling for handholds as they approached the sound which still sounded eerily across the mountains. Just as dawn broke, they reached a large cave and stopped to rest.

Without warning, the wind blew through the entrance of the cave, down the passageways and all around them, causing the deep roar that had summoned them. Kurgaz roared in turn, but this time with laughter, and soon the whole of his guard had tears running down their cheeks. 'It is a sign from Grungni,' he said, 'To show us how to laugh even in such times as these, and to show us a safe haven.' And with that he set about exploring his new domain.

Over the years the caverns have been greatly enlarged, and the winds still blow through the Hornhall of Karak-Hirn. Cleverly constructed doors, valves and hollows amplify the sound just so, and cunningly set fires draw the air through the sounding chambers so that the mountain itself can be sounded to call the warriors to battle or scare away Trolls.

Now as I said, young Alrik is even more traditional than his father Ranulf, and his armies are a sight to make an old warrior glad. But there's more to him than that. For he has taken Karak-Hirn's Book of Grudges and sought with single-minded dedication to erase every slight. To this end he campaigns against greenskins, Skaven, or Elves and extracts a payment in blood for their past misdeeds. It is often that you hear of how our kin have been badly mistreated, but few seek vengeance like Alrik. He would erase every grudge ever held by his clan, and if he lives long enough by Grungni he'll do it. Already he carries one of the volumes of the Book, completely scoured of unpaid blood-debts. This alone fills his followers with boundless hope, as it does me and should you."

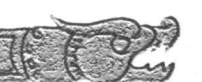

KING ALRIK RANULFSSON

	M	WS	BS	S	T	W	I	A	Ld
Alrik & Bearers	3	7	4	4	5	5	4	6	10

Alrik is the King of Karak-Hirn and is borne into battle on a great shield carried by his loyal followers. He can be taken as a Lord choice in a Dwarf army, but also uses up one of your army's Hero choices. He must be fielded exactly as presented here, and no extra equipment or rune items can be bought for him. The cost of his rune items and Shield Bearers is included in his total cost.

Alrik and his Royal Shield Bearers are treated as a single model with the profile given above. If he fights with a unit he is placed with his Bearers in the centre of the front rank. Note that when in a unit he benefits from the Look out, Sir! rule.

Points: 425.

Weapons: The Axe of Retribution.

Armour: Hrappi-klad.

Unit Strength: Alrik and his Shield Bearers are treated as a single model with a Unit Strength of 3.

Lord of the Hold: If Alrik is included in your army he must be your army General.

Shield Bearers: Alrik is carried into battle on the Great Shield of his ancestors. This makes him very easy to see and so friendly Dwarfs within 18" of him may use his Leadership value, rather than those within 12" as normal. The fighting abilities of the Royal Shield Bearers are included in the characteristics for Alrik himself as all three fight as a single model.

Traditional army: Alrik doesn't trust the unusual machineries of the Engineers' Guild and only rarely includes them in his army. If Alrik is in the army then Gyrocopters, Flame Cannons and Organ Guns cost twice the points they do normally. In addition, your army cannot have more models armed with a handgun than a crossbow.

> When I were but a lad, my father, the King, taught me three things:
>
> Never accept a gift from an Elf.
>
> Never trust gold that glistens in darkness.
>
> Never forget a grudge.
>
> On his deathbed I swore to uphold those values to me own dying day, and Grungni willing I will.
>
> King Alrik Ranulfsson of Karak Hirn

RUNE ITEMS

Axe of Retribution: As the Karak-Hirn Dwarfs fight their enemies, the bright flash of silver is easily seen as the Axe of Retribution rises and falls in deadly arcs. Alrik had this axe made especially for his crusade to avenge the wrongs done to his Hold, and he has sworn not to let it rest until they have all been struck from the Book of Grudges.

The Axe of Retribution has been inscribed with the Grudge Rune and the Breaking Rune (see p. 20).

Hrappi-klad: Suits of heavy golden armour are the traditional battle garb of the King of Karak Hirn and his Shield Bearers. They are plain and unadorned in the functional manner of the Dwarfs, but the protection they offer is far greater than any suit of finely filigreed Elven armour.

This heavy armour gives Alrik and his Bearers a 4+ Armour save. It has also been marked with the Rune of Shielding (see page 21).

Kurgaz's Shield: This ancient shield bears a protective magcial rune, but is of tremendous size and is far too heavy to use normally. However, since it is a valued heirloom of their founder, the Kings of Karak-Hirn still take it to battle – nowadays as a fighting platform borne by two of their strongest followers.

The Shield gives Alrik and his Royal Shield Bearers a 5+ Ward save.

Helm of Eagles: The cunningly wrought runes on this ancient battle-helm give the wearer the sharp eyesight of the hunting eagle as he soars above his prey. No lurking assassins can hide from him, nor secrets be held from him whilst he wears this helm.

Alrik can see the details of enemy troops wherever they are on the battlefield. At the start of each Dwarf turn (before declaring charges, etc), Alrik may gaze at one enemy unit. Your opponent must reveal any hidden troops within the unit (such as Assassins or Night Goblin Fanatics) as well as all magic items carried by models within the unit.

Karak-Hirn's Book of Grudges: The Great Book of Grudges, Dammaz Kron, is held by the High King Thorgrim Grudgebearer, but this is not the only such book. In fact, each Hold has their own book, as indeed do many individual Dwarfs. Actually this is only one volume of the many that comprise Karak-Hirn's collection of grudges. However, this is a unique volume because all the grudges described in its pages have been avenged!

In battle, this has the effect of allowing friendly units within 12" of King Alrik to re-roll failed break tests, just like an army standard. However, it is not actually an army standard and therefore gives no combat resolution bonus and cannot be captured by the enemy for extra victory points.

The walls rang to the thunderous clanging of hammers on anvils, the scrape of blades on whetstones and the roar of a hundred furnaces. In the ruddy gloom, the Dwarfs toiled wordlessly, sweat beading their heavy brows. The air was dry and hot, yet each laboured in a heavy jerkin, some of them even still wore their mail, and their hands were covered with heavy gauntlets.

"How do they stand the heat?" asked Logan Beckestroff, envoy for the Elector Count of Averland. The gangly manling stood two feet taller than the smith beside him, his ruffed shirt and embroidered doublet a stark contrast to the plain leather apron of the Dwarf.

"They're Dwarfs," Drokki Snorrison replied gruffly in answer, as if that were answer enough. In contrast to his unadorned work clothes, the Dwarf smith's heavy black beard was intricately plaited and bound with gold bands, tucked into his rope belt to keep it out of harm's way. Dark eyes glittered from under a thick mop of black hair as he looked up at Logan.

"Of course," the man murmured diplomatically, "I should have realised."

"This here's the second foundry level," Drokki continued, ignoring the manling's interruption. He had only been showing the envoy the forges and foundries and workshops for two days, but was beginning to suspect that the flighty Man was getting bored. He mentally shrugged – Men had such short memories and attention spans it was best to drum it home. "Here most of the apprentices work, from the clans of the southern tunnels down to the fifteenth level. I'm in charge of this lot of beardlings, which is why I'm giving you the show around. I'm getting them to make your swords for you."

"You are entrusting our swords, which we are paying good gold for and no small amount, to your apprentices?" Logan asked the question lightly out of tact, yet inside he was furious. How could the Count's personal guard expect to perform well with the work of youngsters and journeymen?

"That's right," Drokki replied curtly.

Logan gritted his teeth for a moment before continuing.

"For the price we are paying, we expect the highest standards of quality," he looked down at the Dwarf's face and was met by a furious scowl.

"Here now, watch your tongue, manling!" the smith snorted, balling his fists onto his hips. "Them swords'll be better than any manling craft, have no worries about that! If you want swords, you'll get sword work. That's no real test of an artisan's skill, no it ain't. Any beardling can slap a sword together in a few days, ain't much craftsmanship in that. Anyhows, we ain't going to use them, not for fighting like you strange manlings. No, apprentices practice on swords, then it doesn't matter. Now, if you wanted a proper weapon like a hammer or axe, then you'd get someone like me doing it. But then you'd pay for my time too, we can't have skilled smiths like me messing about making swords, can we?"

Under the smith's withering glare, combined with the faintness in his head caused by the extreme heat, Logan felt weak and helpless. Perhaps he wouldn't mention this part in his report to the Elector Count.

"Well?" the old Dwarf demanded. "You still want them or not? If you don't best says so now, then you only have to pay for the fifty we made so far."

"A fair offer," Logan started but changed his mind as the scowl deepened even further, "but one I fear I cannot accept" he continued smoothly. "We had a deal, a bargain in fact I believe you called it, and we shall stick to our word."

"Right then," Drokki said, lightening his mood. "Now I'll take you down to the mines where we can discuss the timber contract for our props."

As he led the man through the din and inferno, Drokki had to stop himself chuckling. It had been a close run thing. He'd almost lost the deal. But, as his grandfather taught him, never bargain with a Dwarf in his own home.

THE REALM OF DWARFS

"Before me stood a heavily reinforced iron door. The guard saluted the approaching Ironbeard and, pulling a massive set of keys from his belt, he opened the lock. My first sight of the treasure contained within this chamber came as I saw the Dwarf guard's face reflect the golden light of the room. As the doors opened I was presented with a sight that few will ever behold. To my dying day the image will forever be burned onto my mind. On each wall of the large chamber hung an assortment of weapons, armour and shields. Rack upon rack of axes, hammers and, to my great surprise, swords filled the chamber. These weapons were not run-of-the-mill items either. Many were wrought from only the finest metals and each had been meticulously polished. Hammers of all shapes and sizes lined the racks next to axes the like of which I have never seen. Fantastic emblems of Dwarf images such as dragons or the masks of Grungni and Grimnir shone brightly on the shields.

My eyes were slowly drawn to the far end of the room. On this wall there was arranged but one set of wargear. It was a complete set of armour, including a shield and helmet made from the finest Gromril. The ornate rune cast upon the breastplate of the suit seemed at first to reflect the light of the torches; it was only on close inspection that I realised that it glowed brightly, empowered with some magic source. A great axe hung from the wall. The weapon's blade looked sharper than a razor and not a single notch could be found along its edge. I had little doubt that this axe had seen combat, for runes of battle were engraved upon it. Yet I could not fail to be astounded at the beauty of such a weapon considering its vicious purpose.

Great wings adorned the side of the full face helmet, and I could but only imagine the size of the bird that they had once been attached to. As I left the chamber, the Ironbeard told me how these wings had been taken from a giant eagle which had attacked the High King in the War of Vengeance. The King had slain the beast and its rider in one fell swipe with his mighty axe.

Never again will I see such an armoury, of that I am sure. The Dwarfs have earned a new respect from me as weaponsmiths beyond comparison".

From the memoirs of Leopold Vorwärts, Envoy of the Emperor Boris Goldgather.

THE GATES OF KARAZ-A-KARAK

Karaz-a-Karak, translated into the Human tongue, roughly means 'the Pinnacle of the Mountains'. It is the largest of the Dwarf strongholds and is one of the most magnificent pieces of architecture in the world. Hidden from view by a winding pass that cuts its way through the Worlds Edge Mountains, as you round yet another outcrop on your long trek through the steep treacherous pass the full splendour of the gates of Karaz-a-Karak suddenly looms before you.

The sheer size of the gates will take your breath away, standing at over four hundred feet tall, the gates appear to be carved into the mountainside. A solid flat bastion of stone reaches up to embrace the clouds and if you turn your head towards the sky you can just make out the glint of a multitude of armoured figures patrolling the upper wall. Carved into the gate is the symbol of Valaya, the Dwarf ancestor-goddess. Her image on the gates is said to protect the city from harm and evil magics.

No visitor ever approaches Karaz-a-Karak unannounced. Miles before even a lone traveller reaches the gates his progress will have been spied by the many hidden watchposts that overlook the Everpeak pass. A lone Dwarf in full clan regalia will await you on your arrival. He bears the title of Gatekeeper and it is to him and him alone that you must state your business.

Few these days are allowed access to the great Dwarf city. Once, the gates stood open to all visitors and the Dwarf race was more than welcoming to strangers in their realm. Years of war and devastation have changed that forever and now they do not encourage contact with other races. Should a visitor have good reason, and very good reason only, to enter the kingdom of Karaz-a-Karak, the gatekeeper will knock rhythmically on the door five times with his intricately carved rune hammer then trace the sign of a secret rune into its flat surface. Silvery seams once invisible to even the closest inspection of the smooth granite surface suddenly appear. Seemingly from out of nowhere a doorway no more than four foot high and three foot wide opens.

It has been many centuries since the High King gave instruction to a Gatekeeper to open the main gates. In the year following the terrible earthquake that shook many of the Dwarf realms to their very foundations, Morgrim Ironbeard, the High King of the time, ordered the gates to be closed. This dour period of Dwarf history is known as the Time of Woes. Many of the Dwarf strongholds were under attack from hordes of greenskins and Skaven that flooded out from the caverns to take advantage of the devastation that the earthquake had unleashed on the Dwarfs. In his wisdom the King shut off access to the great city. In doing so he also shut off the Dwarfs from contact with the outside world and it has remained much this way to the current day. The gates are only opened to allow the High King's army to march to war. In the rare event that this happens, the gates are opened in silence with no ceremony. Dwarfs do not celebrate war and a Dwarf army on the march from Karaz-a-Karak, whilst a sight to behold, is a solemn affair.

The gates of the city have only ever been besieged twice in its long history and both times the besiegers have been forced to abandon their attempts. Even the largest of the great war machines that the Orc Warlord Ugrok Beard Burner brought to bear on the gate barely caused an indentation into the thick stone. The Orc Warlord himself realised the futility of trying to break down the gate with the giant battering ram he had constructed, and the Dwarfs sallied forth and destroyed his horde as he lifted the siege. It is said that amongst the defences of the city great rivers of molten lava can be poured from the mouths of the carved stone dragons that sit atop the upper wall of the gate. Also, it is claimed that the hills around the approach to the gates are filled with powerful steam engines, which can cause avalanches and rockslides, and even drop lengths of the path into hidden chasms and crevasses.

All Dwarfs hold hope in their hearts that one day the giant gate of the great stronghold will open once more and that fine Dwarf craftsmanship will once again be available to trade across the world. Until that day the Dwarfs continue to remain safely protected from the outside world, behind the stone fortress that protects their city.

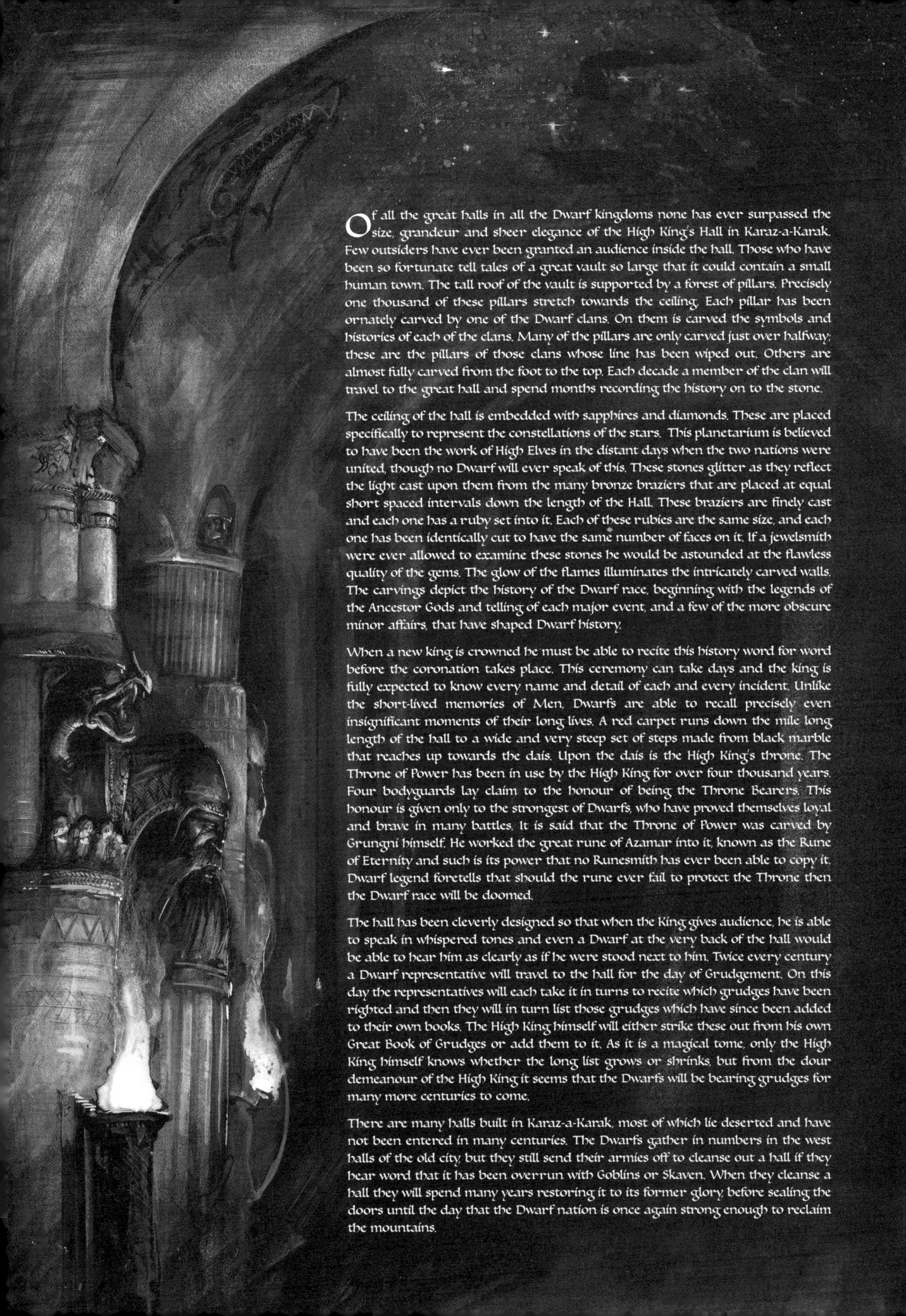

Of all the great halls in all the Dwarf kingdoms none has ever surpassed the size, grandeur and sheer elegance of the High King's Hall in Karaz-a-Karak. Few outsiders have ever been granted an audience inside the hall. Those who have been so fortunate tell tales of a great vault so large that it could contain a small human town. The tall roof of the vault is supported by a forest of pillars. Precisely one thousand of these pillars stretch towards the ceiling. Each pillar has been ornately carved by one of the Dwarf clans. On them is carved the symbols and histories of each of the clans. Many of the pillars are only carved just over halfway; these are the pillars of those clans whose line has been wiped out. Others are almost fully carved from the foot to the top. Each decade a member of the clan will travel to the great hall and spend months recording the history on to the stone.

The ceiling of the hall is embedded with sapphires and diamonds. These are placed specifically to represent the constellations of the stars. This planetarium is believed to have been the work of High Elves in the distant days when the two nations were united, though no Dwarf will ever speak of this. These stones glitter as they reflect the light cast upon them from the many bronze braziers that are placed at equal short spaced intervals down the length of the Hall. These braziers are finely cast and each one has a ruby set into it. Each of these rubies are the same size, and each one has been identically cut to have the same number of faces on it. If a jewelsmith were ever allowed to examine these stones he would be astounded at the flawless quality of the gems. The glow of the flames illuminates the intricately carved walls. The carvings depict the history of the Dwarf race, beginning with the legends of the Ancestor Gods and telling of each major event, and a few of the more obscure minor affairs, that have shaped Dwarf history.

When a new king is crowned he must be able to recite this history word for word before the coronation takes place. This ceremony can take days and the king is fully expected to know every name and detail of each and every incident. Unlike the short-lived memories of Men, Dwarfs are able to recall precisely even insignificant moments of their long lives. A red carpet runs down the mile long length of the hall to a wide and very steep set of steps made from black marble that reaches up towards the daïs. Upon the daïs is the High King's throne. The Throne of Power has been in use by the High King for over four thousand years. Four bodyguards lay claim to the honour of being the Throne Bearers. This honour is given only to the strongest of Dwarfs, who have proved themselves loyal and brave in many battles. It is said that the Throne of Power was carved by Grungni himself. He worked the great rune of Azamar into it, known as the Rune of Eternity and such is its power that no Runesmith has ever been able to copy it. Dwarf legend foretells that should the rune ever fail to protect the Throne then the Dwarf race will be doomed.

The hall has been cleverly designed so that when the King gives audience, he is able to speak in whispered tones and even a Dwarf at the very back of the hall would be able to hear him as clearly as if he were stood next to him. Twice every century a Dwarf representative will travel to the hall for the day of Grudgement. On this day the representatives will each take it in turns to recite which grudges have been righted and then they will in turn list those grudges which have since been added to their own books. The High King himself will either strike these out from his own Great Book of Grudges or add them to it. As it is a magical tome, only the High King himself knows whether the long list grows or shrinks, but from the dour demeanour of the High King it seems that the Dwarfs will be bearing grudges for many more centuries to come.

There are many halls built in Karaz-a-Karak, most of which lie deserted and have not been entered in many centuries. The Dwarfs gather in numbers in the west halls of the old city but they still send their armies off to cleanse out a hall if they hear word that it has been overrun with Goblins or Skaven. When they cleanse a hall they will spend many years restoring it to its former glory before sealing the doors until the day that the Dwarf nation is once again strong enough to reclaim the mountains.

-2005 In the spring of this year the Dwarf trader Gorri Dustbrow was murdered and his wares stolen by the treacherous Elves. For this unforgivable act we will take vengeance on the so called Fair Folk.

-2005 In Dweraki Grugni-Naggrun the Dwarf settlement of Mingol Norn was found burned to the ground. Arrows of Elven design were found amongst the dead. For this we shall ne'er forgive the sons of Bel-Shanaar.

-2005 The murderous Elves who did kill the people of Mingol Norn were found a short way down the track. They denied any wrong doings but guilt was deemed written upon their faces and so they did suffer the penalty of death for their misdoings.

-1997 Word has reached us that we are to gather the clans unto arms. The ambassador of King Gotrek Starbreaker did return from his mission of good will with his beard shaven by the people of Ulthuan. For this wrong we shall not cease until every head is sheared from the shoulders of each and every Elf.

-1974 Woe be it written that Prince Snorri has been slain by the dark hand of an Elf King. Let this misdeed be avenged afore any more grudges weigh the Dwarf nation with grief.

-1968 Let it be recorded that members of our very own clan hath aided in the settlement of the murder of the Prince. For at the battle of Oeragor did our clan's warriors fight and 'twas there did the Elf Lord Imladrik righteously meet his doom.

-1948 Let the burning of our neighbours at Mingol Norn be accounted for. The good news that the vile city of Athel Maraya has been put to the torch did reach us today. For that we owe Morgrim a debt.

-1560 Let it be recorded that on the fourth day of Smirnikul Odroraki the Elven host did leave the old world to return to their accursed shores. With the demise of the Elf King Caledor, the High King has claimed his crown in recompense. Let it be said that grudges outstanding against the Elves are now but a few though let their treachery never be forgiven.

-1500 Lest they ever be forgotten, we record herein the names of those clans which have perished during the great cataclysm. The Dwarfs of the Blacktash, Hit-hammers and Fire-brands will never again walk the mountain passes. Forever shall they be remembered. Word has also reached us that the Undgrim is impassable.

-1499 Word has reached us that our cousins in the hold of Karak Ungor hath lost their ancestral home to Grobi. We shall offer them place to stay 'til that time when they shall reclaim their hold and put the vile greenskins to pay for their foul actions.

-1494 On the ninth day in the month of Sizraki Grimnir-Brur the hordes attacked our own hold. We have beaten successive waves off, yet still more attempt to breach our defences. For this act we shall seek retribution.

-1490 The greenskins have all but been fought off but, with the breaking of the siege, word has reached us about the fall of Karak Varn and the loss of the great mines at Ekrund. For their evil we shall not rest until each Grobi has his head on a stake outside the taken citadels.

-1469 Let it be recorded that the Dwarfs of Karak Izor have requested the use of five of our finest steamrollers. This favour we grant only to open up a communication with our neighbours.

-1456 Our jewelsmiths mourn the loss of Gadrin Holheart who is said to have fallen in the defence of the gold mines at Gunbad. We shall cast a ring of the purest gold inset with the finest Byrnduraz stone to mark his passing. He who brings those responsible for his death to justice shall bear the honour to wear the ring.

-1366 With the fall of Karaz Silverspear, our cousins in the east have fallen in dire need of help. Alas, we have troubles of our own: our routes to the strongholds have become treacherous and many are the number of Orcs and Grobi whom we shall bring to pay for their foul deeds. We have lost seven ore trains to attacks from the murderous creatures.

-1245 Hear the revelations that Karak-a-Karaz has beaten off an invading horde of vile beasts. Many ogres and trolls did fall under Dwarf axe. May they pass by our gates so we can repay them for their years of evil doing. Messages have reached us that the Hall of our ancestor, Barik Axebearer, has been reclaimed. We owe much gratitude to the Dwarfs of King Morgrim Blackbeard for their valiant efforts and hold hope within our hearts that we can soon pay homage at the shrine.

-1201 Today is a day of great celebration. A trade treatise has been made with our neighbours in the hold of Karak Izor. In return for one thousand tonnes of copper ore we shall be sending them two hundred tonnes of iron.

-1190 Kadrin Redmane has left our hold in search of vengeance upon the swarms of Skaven that have soiled the tunnels of Karak Varn.

-1185 Let it be noted that we have avenged the deaths of those who fell to the blades of Grobi and Skaven at Karak Varn. Kadrin Redmane will forever be recorded in our histories as he who claimed a grudge.

-1136 Woe of days that I must record the murder of Kadrin Redmane. Though over thirty Orcs lay at his feet, thrice that number shall we reap vengeance upon before we could even begin to pay him the honour that he is due.

-1101 In celebration of the hundred years of trade between ourselves and Karak Izor the wedding of our own Prince Gumli and the princess Dertain has been arranged.

-1101 So offended was Prince Gumli by the appearance of Princess Dertrain that she has been sent back to Karak Izor. 'Tis recorded that she had a face like a troll chewing a rock. We have kept her dowry as recompense for the wrongs that our eyes had to endure.

-975 Today is a day of mourning, Prince Furgil Morgrimson of Karak-a-Karaz breathes no more. He was slain in a brave attempt to clear the lower halls of Karak Ungor from Skaven. Many thousand are the rats that we shall destroy in his name.

-750 Word has come from the south that vast numbers of goblins have gathered at Karak Azgal. We shall be sending our clans to aid them in this time of trouble.

-739 Our clans have returned jubilant. Many are the number of Grobi that have fallen to their axes. Many more are the numbers that we need to purge before we can once again hold our heads high in honour of the fallen.

-618 The Dwarfs of Karak Izor have still to return our steamrollers. We have sent word that we demand their return but have had no reply back.

Translated from the Book of Grudges of Clan Kamerad.

BARAK VARR

Barak Varr, or 'the Gate to the Sea' is unique amongst the Dwarf strongholds. Approaching from the land there is no indication at all of the busy port that lies ahead. In fact, even standing on the cliff edge it seems to the unsuspecting eye that the ships are destined to smash themselves into the cliff face. The powerful tides of the Black Gulf have carved out a deep cave system into the tall white cliffs. Here in these vast sea caverns the Dwarfs harbour their trading fleet. The stronghold of Barak Varr is small in comparison to the other strongholds that tunnel deep into the Worlds Edge Mountains, but the Dwarfs of the Hold enjoy a relatively cosmopolitan lifestyle, and are less dour and introverted than other Dwarfs. Not only is it one of the few strongholds that has remained open to traders from other nations, but the Dwarfs of Barak Varr are renowned for their hospitality. It is said that a Dwarf breakfast is a feast large enough to fill even the belly of the plumpest Halfling. Dwarfs have a strong dislike for water and the Dwarfs at Barak Varr are unusual in that some of them become sailors. Even so, they still do not relish setting foot on flimsy wooden ships which could easily break up in a strong gale. They put their faith in huge iron constructions driven by paddles powered by steam boilers which are located deep within the armoured hulls of these vessels, the workings of which are kept secret by the Dwarf engineers.

Traders of every realm, from Araby to Lustria, gather together at Barak Varr, knowing that they can expect the legendary hospitality of the Dwarfs to refresh them on their arrival. Amongst the most famous locations within Barak Varr is the White Pony tavern where they stock a variety of beers and spirits from all around the known world, and a traveller can spend days there without ever sampling a drink twice. In the market area of the port a visitor can buy anything, from fine Araby silks to exotic Lustrian statues, Halfling mixed spices to fertility charms from the Southlands.

Because it is tunnelled into the cliffs the stronghold is almost impervious to attack by land. More than one nation has tried to assault Barak Varr by sea in the past, but the immense firepower of the Dwarf fleet has always driven away enemy armadas. Combined with the many cannons whose barrels bristle from revetments along the cliff face, an enemy fleet has to be very brave to approach the stronghold. Only a fool fights a fort.

Although it is strictly located in the lands of the Border Princes, this is diplomatically ignored by the estranged Dukes and Barons, as the stronghold protects them from invasion. The generosity favoured to the Dwarfs also extends to the Dwarfs' free passage along the many trade routes that lead through the Border Princes. If truth be known, the Dwarfs inhabited the Border Princes long before any other race laid claim to the land and probably constructed the roads themselves. It is in fact the Dwarfs who put up with the presence of Men in their ancestral realm purely because there is very little mineral wealth to be mined from the lands.

From the east pass of Karaz-a-Karak I began my trek along the Silver Road. Most passes to the east of the Worlds Edge Mountains are dangerous routes and within a few miles of leaving the vicinity of the Dwarf stronghold I found my path difficult to travel. Night Goblin tribes and Orc bandits have claimed ownership of the eastern half of the Worlds Edge Mountain range and will attack any intruders. I was reliably informed that the Silver Road was the safest route to the east since the Dwarfs have managed to hold most of the surrounding mountains. Once the route was well travelled. My guide told me that vast mule trains permanently trekked back and forth along the road carrying loads of silver ore on their backs, from which some scholars believe the road's name originates.

The route descends steeply through the Deadrock Gap where even Dwarfs are now hesitant to go. It was here that my guide left me to return to the safety of his Hold. I carefully made my way down the slope, losing only one mule on the treacherously narrow path. As well as the usual tribes of Goblins that now inhabit the ruins of Mount Silverspear, at certain times of the year many Giants gather here. It is largely believed that they group together for some ritualistic ceremony. The intrepid Halfling adventurer, Will Bough, is the only known witness of the ceremony and he paled, refusing to talk of the subject when I began to enquire about his experience. Whatever the dark nature of the gathering, the Giants revel in hurling huge boulders down into the pass at any creatures that should be unfortunate enough to catch their attention. Care should be taken if you intend to travel this route and a sturdy, preferably Dwarf-made, helmet is highly recommended.

Once I safely made it through the Deadrock Gap, the road continued on through the Blasted Wastes. It stretched on into the distance as far as my eye could see. Opinion varies as to the final destination of this road and as to who constructed it and more importantly why. Nonetheless few Dwarfs who have ever travelled the road past Mount Silverspear have ever returned. Of those rare few who have, I found them reluctant to speak of what lies to the east of the Worlds Edge Mountains, cursing in their own tongue and falling silent. It is with trepidation of my journey ahead that I dispatch this scroll by means of a carrier bird. I trust that it reaches you and pray that you will receive another soon.

Your most faithful servant,

Jacob Stachelthorf

I had expected the Underway, or Undgrin as it is known in the Khazalid tongue, to be a treacherous ruined route. My research into the histories of the Dwarf nations led to my belief that it had been virtually destroyed in the Time of Woes. To my great amazement what I found was a road that makes the Street of Sigmar in Altdorf seem like a farm track in comparison. Wide enough for two cavalry regiments to pass each other with ease, the Undgrim is truly spectacular. I hired a guide to escort me to my destination of Karak Kadrin, although I plan to make a detour to encompass a visit to Zhufbar on route.

My guide informed me on some of the history of the Undgrin. It would seem that it was constructed in the time of the High King Snorri Whitebeard. Originally it was designed to link the northern strongholds with those of the south, as the winding treacherous mountain routes proved to exact a high toll on Dwarf ore shipments. As trade began to flourish, the Dwarfs saw a need to expand the route. A series of routes were added to the main road, 'Umwan' in Khazalid, linking each of the major Dwarf settlements together. Before the great earthquakes, the Dwarf engineers had even constructed a gigantic steam driven wagon which pulled carts filled with ore up and down the route.

Unfortunately all this was destroyed in the Time of Woes. The great earthquakes collapsed many of the sections of the Undgrin and blocked off communications between the strongholds. Most of the mountain passes had been usurped by Goblins and were no longer safe to travel, and thus the strongholds found themselves isolated and vulnerable to attack.

It was with this in mind that I expected to find a ruinous rocky route but my expectations were proved wrong. The Dwarfs have rebuilt much of the northern section of the Umwan and many of its tributary roads. Every twenty feet a massive oil torch burns, lighting up the busy route. Gigantic pillars reach up one hundred feet to the ceiling of the Underway, which is so smoothly hewn from the rock that it reflects the light of the torches. Many engineers are busy constructing areas of the route, though what they are actually doing I can but speculate. Most of those engineers whom we passed were busy in conversation and seemed little concerned by the disruption that their work caused.

More carts than I have ever laid eyes upon travel the Undgrim, all laden with precious ores and gemstones.

As I passed some tributary routes, I took note that they were blocked off from access and many had guards posted at their entrances. These, my guide informed me, were sections that are still ruinous. Many of these routes are occupied by hordes of Skaven and Goblins who took advantage of the earthquakes to take them over. From what my guide told me, I gathered that it is the Dwarfs' highest priority to clear these sections of vermin and to once again link all of the Dwarf Holds. Should they achieve this, I have little doubt that once again the Dwarf nation will flourish.

Your most faithful servant,

Jacob Stachelthorf

THE JOURNAL OF JACOB STACKELDHORF.
TRAVELS THROUGH THE WORLDS EDGE MOUNTAINS.

DAY 29. I have begun my trek up Karaz Whitecap. I find myself having to regularly stop for breath. The air as we ascend the mountain grows thin and I cannot walk for more than an hour before I must stop. My Dwarf guide is most patient with me, although I have little doubt that such is the vigour and stamina of these stout fellows that he could easily have reached the top by now without any need for rest. We have made camp for the evening at a beautiful site that overlooks the great lake of Black Water. In the distance I can just make out the ruins of Cragmere. From this high vantage point, had I not known of the beasts and monsters that now inhabit the former stronghold, I would have thought it no different from any other of the great Holds.

Day 30. My sleep was disturbed by the bellows of the stone trolls that stalk the mountainsides. Many was the time I woke believing the strong winds that buffeted my tent in the night to be my impending doom at the claws of one of these monstrous creatures. By noon we had reached the top of the mountain. My legs gave way to the sight before me. A bridge arcs high between the peaks of Karaz Whitecap and Karag Fanghorn. I cannot even hazard a guess at how the Dwarfs built such a structure, or why. I can now understand why the Dwarfs call this bridge 'Ekrund Grom' or the Stair of Courage. My guide has informed me that we shall not be making the crossing today as the winds are too strong. I thank Sigmar for his mercy, but know that this is a brief respite before I must search my heart to summon the courage to cross.

DAY 31. A party of troll slayers have arrived at the summit. Usually loners, they have gathered together to perform a rite of passage for one of their number. For some unknown reason, trolls' guts acquired from a recent victorious battle were tied to his ankles. What happened next was beyond my comprehension. He walked to the centre of the bridge carrying a large boulder to which was tied the other end of the length of troll gut. Placing the boulder he then jumped off the bridge to what I thought was his doom. Amazingly the troll guts are so tough they took his weight and he was catapulted back up towards the bridge. After retrieving their comrade the small party offered me the chance to undertake this ritual, but I value my life more than these strange caste of Dwarfs and politely declined.

DAY 32. Today I finally summoned up the courage to cross the skybridge. My guide informed me that I was the first Man to do so since Sigmar himself. I must admit though it was not easy to do. The bridge is wide enough to accomodate severel Dwarfs abreast at its start, but by the time I had traversed its path to the centre it becomes barely a few feet wide. I was very glad to reach the other side and start my descent to the stronghold of Karak Kadrin where I intend to visit the famed Slayer Shrine. After finally meeting some of this legendary caste, albeit in such strange circumstances, I will regard these doomed Dwarfs with a new respect.

To his most venerable Lord Duregar,

I trust this message meets you strong in mind and wide in girth.

Tis a welcome change that I may send you news of our fortune, yet rejoice not early as though the message I send is of great tidings, the time of celebration has yet to pass. I will remind you of our last communication though I know I need not do so. My clan had spent many years gathering strength in preparation to march south. It was with high spirits that we set forth on the ancient pass. Once again the kinsfolk of Lunn were eager to feel the soil of our homeland beneath our boots. Far too many centuries had passed since Dwarf eyes had fallen upon Vala-Azrilungol.

The journey was swift and neither grobi nor gronti barred our way. We entered the basin where once the city stood proud and tall, via the pass that winds its way around Kvinn-Wyr. The sight of the fortifications, though they lay in ruinous form, stirred each warrior's heart with a passion that even I have never felt before.
A murmur grew up from the army and could not be quelled.

I wish I could claim that our route down the northern approach to the Karad was met with the same joy, but the vile grobi totems of poor hapless adventurers brought down our spirits. Their skulls now hailed our arrival and brought swift reminder of the dangers we faced.

As we passed through the ruins of the north gate a tide of black-robed night goblins poured from the walls and amassed before us. Forming into solid shieldwalls, my warriors prepared for their onslaught. Crazed fanatics fuelled by toxic fungi took a heavy toll of many of my kinsfolk, as did the vicious cave squigs whose huge teeth tore through even our strongest armour. Huge boulders crashed down upon our ranks and great spears were launched into our midst, yet with stout courage did the proud army hold fast.

We met the charge of the vile grobi whose numbers tripled that of our small band. Wave after wave of gibbering greenskins sallied from the ruins, but in our hearts we knew vengeance was at hand. With the names of our fallen forefathers on our lips each Dwarf amongst our clan took revenge. By evening there was not one greenskin who could draw breath remaining within the city walls.

As I write this message my warriors and engineers are hastily constructing a barricade around the inner wall. Once word has spread you can be sure as gold shines and elves lie that many more grobi will gather to try to retake what is not theirs to possess. Already my sentries have spied movement amongst the debris that litters what was once the outer walls.

If we are to stand any chance of holding our position within the city then we will need reinforcements. The time to reclaim the southern holds is at hand but lies not within my power alone to do so.

My kin already owe you more than we can ever repay for your generous hospitality in letting us take refuge in Karaz-a-Karak. If you could send any help to aid us in this time of need then one day I can but dream that the proud city of Karak Eight Peaks can repay your friendship.

Honourably yours

Beleragond

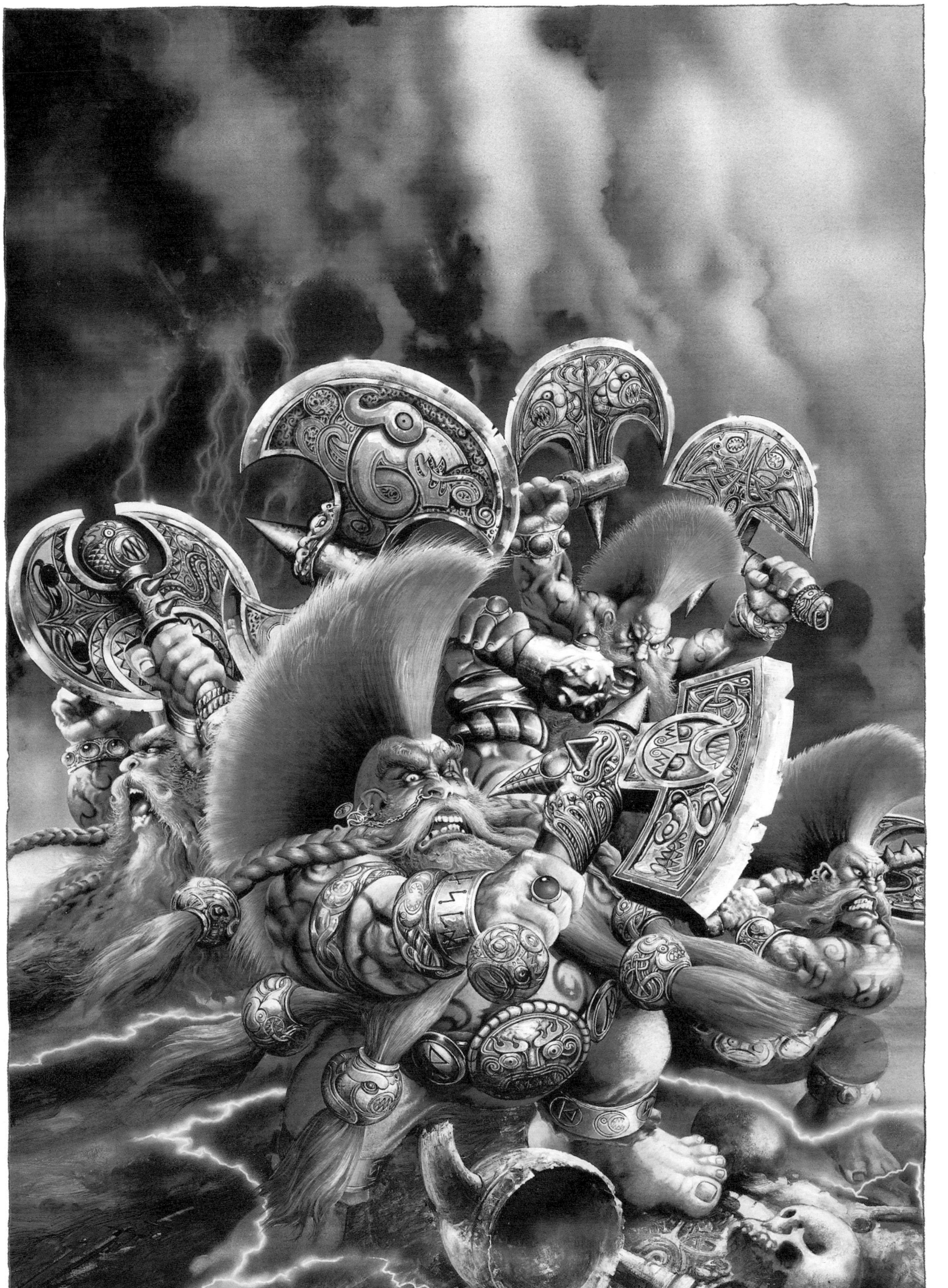

KARAK AZGAL

In its heyday the City of Jewels, Karak Izril in the Dwarf tongue, formed perhaps the most extravagant Hold that has ever been built. Once ranked amongst the largest Dwarf settlements, whose wealth exceeded that of even Karak-a-Karaz, this fortune would ultimately lead to its downfall. Built within a mountain range that contained particularly large deposits of a variety of gemstones, it is said that such was the wealth in the city that every Dwarf house had a large gem as its doorknob. With the fall of Karak Eight Peaks many of the trade routes to the other Dwarf strongholds were opened to the Orcs. Taking full advantage of this, the Orcs, already encouraged by their victory, poured through these passes and assaulted the neighbouring Holds.

Even the Orcs had heard of the wealth of Karak Izril and flocked to breach its sturdy gates. The attack caught the fortress by surprise and was orchestrated with an intense ferocity fuelled by greed for the Dwarfs' gemstones. The greenskins amassed on the north wall. This section of the fortress had particularly weak defences as the Dwarfs in their pride had thought Karak Eight Peaks, which faced this wall, would never fall. Following the destruction of Karak Eight Peaks the Skaven had begun to swarm into the Southern Mountains. The Skaven masses had for many years been tunnelling into the deepest Dwarf gem mines, and their leaders decided to use the Orc attack to their advantage. The Dwarfs of Karak Izril found themselves under attack from their weak north wall and from the mines below. Faced on two weak flanks by far superior numbers, the Dwarfs knew that they stood no chance of saving the city, but Dwarfs would rather die than give up their treasure.

The Dwarf defenders gathered in a deep vault and it was here they made their stand against the massed attack from both Skaven and Orcs hungry for Dwarf blood. As the last Dwarf fell the Orc general realised that the defence of the vault had been a clever ruse. The moment the Orcs breached the wall and poured into the city, a small unit of Engineers, accompanied by the Runelord Stormbeard, had carried the treasures to a separate vault away from the main city and sealed up the vast hoard in the cave. Whilst the doomed Dwarf warriors sold their lives dearly to gain time, Stormbeard had inscribed special Runes of Hiding

THE REALM OF DWARFS

so that only he would ever know of the exact location of the door to the treasure. The Dwarfs vowed to return and what better incentive than an enormous pile of precious stones. On leaving the doomed city, the Runelord renamed the once grand stronghold Karak Azgal or 'Hoard Peak'.

After the destruction of Karak Azgal, the dragon Graug the Terrible made his nest within the ruins. Dragons have a unique ability to smell gold and precious stone and so Graug soon discovered the vault. These monstrous creatures attract a mate through the size of their treasure hoard, and Graug added to the already vast hoard over the following centuries.

Where there lies treasure and dragons there also follow adventurers and treasure seekers. Many expeditions were sent by the Dwarf jewelsmith's guild, but it was a young beardling by the name of Skalf who finally discovered the lost vault and slew the dragon. His descendants have used the wealth to build up a small fortress within the ruined city. This small stronghold has become a haven for adventurers to strike out in exploration of the Goblin infested ruins. Ever since Karak Eight Peaks was retaken, the Dwarfs hold out against attack in this remote outpost in the hope that one day soon the southern Holds will flourish once again.

For Skalf he was but short in size, in courage towered high,
Unto the lair of Graug he stepped, no fear lest he should die.
Fortune blessed him with her kiss, for thus the beast it slept,
Over gold and rainbow stone, the youngest Dwarf he crept.
The bones of Men of virtue high lay scattered where they fell,
For honour had they met their death, did noble lives they sell.
For many centuries had the dragon lain upon its cache,
Little did the dread wyrm dream that it had met its match.
In his hand the young Dwarf bore an ancient runic blade,
Upon the open neck of Graug, the deepest cut it made.
In the cavern did it rain a shower of gem and gold
As ancient beast formed dance of death, slain by a Dwarf so bold.
Dragonslayer and his kin did city lay their claim,
In Karak Azgal to this day do Skalf Clan Dwarfs remain.
To seek a fortune, risking death a small toll must you pay,
But fare ye strong in courage then to Azgal make your way.

Verse 24, taken from 'The Fall of the Southern Holds', a traditional Dwarf song recanted on the eve of the fall of Karak Eight Peaks.

DWARFS AT WAR

Sagely Advice Given to King Alrik when a Young Dwarf Prince.

"As King, upon your shoulders will fall the task of making war upon the enemies of the Hold. These foes are many and varied, from the numerous barbaric Orcs to the devious Elf folk. There are two reasons to wage war, and two alone. The first is to protect the Hold from invasion and to safekeep its lands and the passage of your subjects among your realm. The second is to restore honour in the Hold, whether it be for an unpaid debt, an oath sworn or to demand reparation from those who have wronged us. These are the only reasons to take up the axe, to don the battlegear of your ancestors. Never must you wage war for personal gain, out of jealousy, spite or other low feelings.

As in all things, war must be done honourably, for though other races may slink and crawl and be treacherous and insincere, only by adhering to the traditions and tenets of your forefathers will you be able to meet them in the Halls of Grimnir when he calls your name. Dishonour your clan and your Hold and there shall be no respite for you, and the dragon's flame will torment you for eternity. Thus did Grimnir speak at the dawn of time, and thus shall it be forever after.

To protect your home and the homes of your subjects, there are many strategies and contingencies of war that you can employ. If the force is inferior, seek them out on the mountainsides, use your knowledge of the hills and rocks and high passes to bring you to an advantage over the enemy, and then await their arrival. Greet them with the roar of cannons and the hail of the crossbow, and bright shall the sun shine on your axes and hammers.

Once you have driven them off, however, be cautious and hold your ground. A rash pursuit may lead you into a disadvantage, where an enemy may lie in wait. Better to hold and repel than to flounder into danger.

If the force arrayed against you is great, then the mountains and your Hold itself are your best weapons. Withdraw within your gates and bastions; there is no shame in saving Dwarf lives, and it is a great crime to have your kin slain because of foolish pride. Our stone walls have endured for generations, neither Man nor Orc nor Elf have breached their defences, and none ever shall. Pour upon their heads the molten metal from the forges, and dash their engines of siege to pieces with rocks and cannon balls. Use the underground paths to strike at their rear, and send discord and fear through their ranks. Destroy their war engines, such as they might have, burn their baggage and scatter their livestock so that they will hunger and thirst and lose the heart for battle. Only when they have scattered should you venture forth, to clear away any stragglers and remove the last vestiges of their presence from your lands, but remember the lesson of due caution, and drive not your army far from your gates lest the enemy unexpectedly gather and relaunch their assault, catching you unawares.

If you must, by dint of oath and duty, wage war upon a foreign land then remember these words well. In comparison to the hordes of Orcs and the teeming masses of mankind, we are few, and to attack them in much force would require you to leave your Hold undefended. This is unforgivable, so when marching to war in others' realms muster what force you must and march with all haste. Win the battle and return to your defence, for others have eyes and ears and will see your brave warriors march forth and hear their boots upon the passes and may decide that you are weak and vulnerable.

Except against an isolated fastness, it is a waste of Dwarf lives to dash your army upon the walls of the enemy, shoddily built as they may seem. Instead, take up a position close to the passes and highways that he must use for commerce and military expedition, so that nothing shall pass. Choose a position that is well defensible and await your enemy's attack. A hill overlooking a town is good, from where your war engines can hurl shot upon his people and force him to show his hand, or the sides of a valley where he must pass his armies through and so must clear your army from its place before he can defend other parts of his kingdom. When he attacks, await him in full force, let him waste his strength upon your armour while you punish him for his assault with crossbow, handgun, stone thrower and flame cannon.

Be wary of your warriors dashing from the cover of your engines and missile fire, for, sturdy as they are, a faster foe will outflank them and come upon the undefended engines, or they shall become surrounded and cut off from aid or retreat.

If your foe be a coward or weakling and does nothing to protect his lands or people from the threat of your force, you have but one option. You must then, and not before, march upon him with your warriors and force him to do battle, beating upon his door with your axes and hammers if need be. In such a force, you must return your engines of war to the Hold, for you must often march hard and far, and these engines will not only slow your warriors but will provide targets for ambush.

Unfettered by defending your engines, your warriors can drive into the heart of the opposing force and bring them to dreadful battle. Seek out the hardest of his units, for they will be no match for you and your veterans, but march as a single army; do not scatter your warriors hither and thither for they should fight as a whole and not be unsupported. Crush his regiments in turn, turning the full force of your army upon them, until they are lying upon the ground or scattered to the hills.

If the enemy surrenders, temper your treatment by their conduct and that of their peoples. If they fought bravely and with honour, as some Men on occasion may do, then you can be lenient and simply demand reparations for the expense of your war. If, like the Grobi and the followers of the dark gods, they are beneath contempt then feel no remorse if you slay them out of hand, for no good can come of sparing them. Elf folk should not be executed, though harsh imprisonment and hardship is well deserved, for on occasion ransom can be demanded from their King for their return, as is right for they still owe us much for what they stole during the War of Vengeance. Others you may fight, and upon your judgement lies this burden, but remember always that Grimnir and your ancestors watch you.

Upon the execution of the battle, return with all speed to your home. Dally not on the field to glorify with prideful triumph, but see to the defence of the Hold. Victory celebrations are permitted, according to ancient ceremony and tradition, but first always observe the proper rites for those who will fight no more, for they shall never again celebrate alongside you until you are ushered to the Hall of Grimnir. Then upon the anvils and in the furnaces must you repair your battle gear, for, though you may win a victory, ever are there fools in this world who will rise to challenge your might again. So fought your father and his father and your forefathers before them, and so fight should you."

-513 Alas these are dangerous times for our empire. King Lunn is currently bound for Karak-a-Karaz with the news that Karak Eight Peaks has fallen into enemy hands. I fear lest the horde take control of the southern strongholds.

-469 Our fears were truly founded. I wish that I could strike out this day from our records but to do so would dishonour those who fell in defence of our realm. Goblins do defile our temples and halls all about the south. Before he died from a wound in the back from a grobi arrow, the messenger told us that Karak Izril and Karak Drazh have fallen to the foul greenskin. There was no word of Karak Azul but we can but fear the worst. The days when we could hope to avenge those who fell to Orcs and their kind are disappearing, but still we shall fight on to avenge the dead.

-380 Though it is known that we shall never cease to slay Orcs and grobi, let it be noted that this month they started a new account with our kind that shall only be repaid with the blood of the last goblin. 'Tis said that the High King Logan Proudbeard has been taken prisoner by Orc-kind.

-379 The King has been saved and many are the Orcs who hath been driven from Karak-a-Karaz. 'Tis said that at Black Water a host of green has fled from the shores. We have sent our rangers into the mountains in the event that those who choose to hide within our mountain will be dissuaded from making home in our land.

-378 The surrounding area has been all but purged of every Orc. Many gathered to regroup here but our rangers' crossbows soon paid off a few grudges and, though small are the number that we may strike off our list, great is the pleasure in doing so.

-245 We have opened up a trade negotiation with Mankind. I found them a slow witted race. Still, any enemy of Grobi will find friendship amongst our people.

-108 An expedition has been sent forth to recover the treasures lost at Karak Azgal. Led by the bravest of our warriors, Daled Stormbreaker, we can but wish them luck on their enterprise.

-20 At last the Dwarfs of Karak Izor have sent back our steamrollers. Let it be recorded that they have been sent back in poor condition. As a result we have closed our trade accounts with that Karak.

-15 Strange are the events that pass. King Kurgan was captured by Orcs but he was rescued by Mankind. Today we received proclamation that a treatise has been reached between Prince Sigmar of the Unberogen tribe and the great Dwarf nation.

-1 The clans have returned from war at the nearby Black Fire Pass. The victorious horns heralded their arrival. Together, Dwarf and Man look to forge an alliance that will drive greenskin from the west. Many are those that can rest in their tombs tonight, for many are the grudges that hath been settled in greenskin blood.

18 Thane Grodrik has noted a grudge against Thane Barin for insults made against his Aunt Brodrika at the wedding of Thane Barin.

708 King Fodrin Axegirth has been said to have dishonoured our own King by saying he is "petty minded". For this insult the King has ordered that communication between the two Karaks cease. He also insisted it be recorded that we ceased communication first.

1032 Alas the news that we have long suspected to be true has been verified. The shield and axe of Daled Stormbreaker hath been recovered from the lair of the wyrm Graug. Yet fortuitous is the news that the hero's death has been avenged by Skalf the Dragonslayer.

1098 A feud between the Grimbul Clan and the Drakki Clan has started. Thane 'Everlate' Grimbul has refused to return a forge bellows to Thane Drakki, borrowed by his grandfather.

1111 A terrible illness has run through our halls and homes. The King himself lies feverish on his bed. It is with solemn heart that I fill his book.

1112 Alas the King has died. I find little comfort to write that his death has not been in vain. We found many Skaven burrowing beneath our Hold, but few remain to spread any more of the foul plague that has taken many Dwarfs to their grave.

2010 Once again Dwarf and Man unite. This time we fight off the evil of undeath that is afflicting the lands around us. Dwarf cannon forged within the heart of our own Hold soon brought the walls of Castle Tempelhof down. So, we pay debt to those of our kin who disappeared to appease the dark thirst of these creatures.

2303 Many brave warriors have we lost to bands of marauders who have poured out from the north. I have no doubt that many more will fall to the foul Chaos Gods before war is ended.

2321 The Clans Grodrik and Barin have reconciled their differences with a marriage between the renowned hero Smakki Brightaxe and Dunhilda the Fair.

2420 Let the name Grom the Paunch forever be remembered as a name of terror. A goblin horde the likes we have never heard of before has rampaged through the lands. We sent our forces to drive him away but too thick was the green horde that enveloped our warriors. We can but hope that Mankind's new Empire can turn away the invading horde.

2473 Good news comes rarely, but today is a day of celebration for Karak Eight Peaks once again lies in the hands of Dwarfs. 'Tis rumoured that a descendant of King Lunn himself now rules over the hold.

2499 Clan Grimbul have returned the infamous forge bellows and the feud with Clan Drakki is finished.

2503 Let it be remembered that by means of forgotten tunnels, an Orc force led by Gorfang Rotgut has attacked and taken the proud hold of Karak Azul. For the shame and humiliation that the vile horde wrought upon Kadrik, the King's son, we shall renew our efforts to bring all of Orc-kind to pay for their murderous deeds.

2510 Tidings of the defeat of Warlord Gnashrak at the hands of King Ungrim Ironfist bring but a brief respite in our war against the Greenskins. We shall not rest in our slaying of each and every one of them, and only when the ashes of their bones have been dispersed by the winds shall the grudge be settled.

Translated from the Book of Grudges of Clan Kamerad.

DWARFS ABROAD

The might of the Dwarf empire rests in the craggy peaks of the Worlds Edge Mountains, where their legends claim that the Ancestor Gods dug the first Hold. However, in the golden days of the Dwarf realm, they travelled far and wide, seeking new seams of minerals and gems and trading with other races. In this time, a number of Holds were founded across other parts of the Old World.

Dwarfs from outside the Worlds Edge Mountains are regarded with a bit of suspicion by Dwarfs from the older Holds – less respectful of their seniors and tradition, more likely to have truck with other races and tamper with things. Of course, to an outsider there is little difference to discern, although possibly the Dwarfs of the Grey Mountains, Black Mountains and further afield may have a slightly more adventurous spirit. The most hardline Dwarfs of the Worlds Edge Mountains have various words for these outsiders, such as *wanaz* (bad-beards), *zaki* (mad wanderers), *skrati* (poor prospectors) and *garazdrak* (which roughly translates as distant rebels). For their part, the Dwarfs outside the ancestral Holds, as they are sometimes referred to, have a tendency to call their distant kin *grumbaki*, which means grumblers or whiners. Even with this slight animosity, a Dwarf would always put another Dwarf before a person of another race – Dwarf solidarity runs in the blood, and to the outside world there is not much difference between a Dwarf of Karak-Hirn and a Dwarf of Karak-Kadrin.

There are also those Dwarfs whose forefathers wandered even further afield, and settled in more distant or strange lands. To the far north lies Kraka Drak, home of the Norse Dwarfs. So long ago did their ancestors enter the Norscan mountains that these Dwarfs have a different language and customs, something which unites all of the other Holds together. In many respects they share traits and traditions with the Men of Norsca, both in dress, beliefs and behaviour. However, whether this is because they have become more like the Norse, or the Norse have become more like the Dwarfs, is a matter of conjecture and speculation. The Norse Dwarfs are regarded as even madder than other expatriate Dwarfs by many, and much of this is blamed on their Hold's closer proximity to the Chaos Wastes and the Chaos-worshipping humans of the cold and bleak north. Norse Dwarfs are famed even amongst other Holds for their skill at drinking, holding annual quaffing contests to determine the greatest ale-throats. They also reputedly have a peculiar variant of Slayers called 'berserkers' by Men – Dwarfs so grief-stricken and dishonoured that they shave off all of their hair, foam at the mouth and charge into battle determined to hurl themselves into a glorious death on the enemies' weapons.

Over the years, many Dwarfs have also settled in the towns and cities of the Empire and Bretonnia, and even as far as Tilea. Here they do not build Holds, but instead fortified guildhouses can be found, surrounded by a Dwarf quarter where all of the Dwarfs will live. Frequently these houses will have vast cellars and catacombs, so that a small building above ground may well house a considerable clan beneath the surface. Even among such outgoing Dwarfs, old habits die hard.

The services of these Dwarfs are highly prized as engineers, stone masons and mining overseers. It was Dwarfs who first introduced blackpowder to the Empire and helped with the founding of the Nuln Gunnery School and the Imperial College of Engineers. Many of these Dwarfs are considered renegades by the Dwarf Engineers Guild, having been kicked out at a young age for outlandish experiments or for voicing opinions on matters that did not concern them. Others are the descendants of refugees from the captured Holds, lured to human lands by the promise of gold, or unable to face the shame of asking another Hold for sanctuary. These Dwarfs are even more embittered than their kin of the mountains, begrudging the day they were dispossessed, yearning for a chance to reclaim their ancestral lands.

THE WAR OF

"Heed well, stubble-chinned beardlings, while I tell you the tale of the greatest treachery, the most base treason to be inflicted upon us. It was in the reign of Gotrek Starbreaker, four and a half thousands of years ago, when our empire spread across the world and even the poorest Dwarf had a bag of gold the size of your head. At that time, the peoples of the Elf kingdoms and the sons of Grungni lived in peace with one another. Trade flowed across the world, and our coffers filled with well-earned Elf gold as the kin of Ulthuan scrambled to own the labours of our magnificent artisans, whose apprenticeship work surpassed that of today's greatest smiths.

But then the capricious and faithless folk of Ulthuan, dishonourable to an Elf, were overcome by a greed for our lands and possessions. In an act of betrayal never again equalled, they ambushed our convoys, slew our warriors and maidens and stole our finely crafted goods. But Gotrek Starbreaker, being a king of whom it's said wore wisdom and age easily upon his brow, stayed his hand and sent messengers and envoys to the shores of the Elf isle to parley with the folk of distant Ulthuan. In derision were they greeted, and in dishonour were they ejected; their beards, long and lustrous and bushy with age, were shorn from their faces and they were flung from the Elf realms with the cackle of cruel Elf laughter ringing in their ears.

Now, it cannot be said that the sons of Grugni are an impetuous people, for our anger is liken to the fuse of the cannon and burns slowly. But just as assuredly does a cannon fire when the fuse is full burnt, so too does our anger erupt and roar into life and portend great devastation for our enemies.

So our magnificent armies marched, their hearts burning with thoughts of vengeance upon the troublesome Elf folk. Snorri Halfhand, son of King Starbreaker, sought out the host of the Elven Phoenix King and in battle they clashed, solid Dwarf steel against the shoddy weapons of Ulthuan. Great was the slaughter, many kin of Ulthuan regretted their folly that day, but we sons of Grugni paid a high blood price too. Being of noble birth, Snorri deigned to challenge the Elf King, Caledor of the Second, to mortal combat for victory, yet an underhand blow by the vile Elf despatched Snorri, and his army, overcome with woe at this dishonourable deed, scattered from the field of battle.

Snorri's cousin Morgrim was incensed by the death of his kin, and led his folk upon Oeragor. For two days the Elf-kin avoided him, their cowardice outweighing their pride despite the best taunts and ruses of Morgrim. Finally, the two forces met; the glittering white-silver of the Elves against the burnished steel and bronze of Morgrim's great army. The air was filled with the arrows of the Elf-folk, while the bolts of Morgrim's crossbows darkened the skies like a thunderhead. For hours the exchange continued until both sides had exhausted their ammunition. Drawing mighty hammers and axes that burned with runes of vengeance

VENGEANCE

and justice, Morgrim's army marched upon the slender Elf-folk. Morgrim himself, his grey-bearded veterans around him, pushed into the heart of the Elf army, seeking the greatest warrior to face. He found the Elf prince Imladrik and the silent but deadly Swordmasters. Never before had there been such a clash, the swords of the Elf host ringing dully against the finely fashioned armour of Morgrim's kin, whose hammers shed scales and crushed bones with relentless ferocity. Morgrim bested Imladrik, his ancient rune-axe cleaving the thin-blooded prince from midriff to neck, and set the silvered host of the Ulthuan cowards to flight. And this was when an Elf was a proper Elf, not the stringy wastrels you'd fight these days.

Morgrim, honoured with the title of Elgidum the Elfdoom by his lords, implacably pursued the pallid-skinned weaklings, first razing the Elf town of Athel Maraya to its foundations, then besieging the port citadel of Tor Alessi. High King Gotrek Starbreaker, with all the kin of Karaz-a-Karak, joined Morgrim and between them arrayed a vast army of stout warriors from half a dozen Holds. Never since has the world trembled under so many Dwarf boots. As the ironclad legion of the Dwarf King assailed the walls of Tor Alessi, the Elves quailed in their slender towers and thin-walled minarets, so mighty was the force arrayed against them.

For a hundred days the rocks of our catapults made the walls and ground shake, punishing the shoddy workmanship of the Elf city. King Starbreaker, Morgrim Elgidum beside him, breached the gates with his Hammerers and fought his way to the central citadel, where he found the traitorous Elf King Caledor II.

The craven Caledor refused to come out and fight like a true warrior, and the High King thus set about the tower with his great hammer, crushing poorly mortared brick and shattering the flimsy foundations until the tower toppled and Caledor was forced to face him.

Finally spurred by his predicament, the Phoenix King of the Elven Isle drew his long-bladed sword and he and the High King duelled. Long lasted that fight, for although an Elf, Caledor had been tutored in the ways of battle by the best of Ulthuan's warrior-sages. Yet Gotrek was no beardless whelp, and neither could land a blow upon the other. Finally, as night began to draw its veil over the ruined city, sturdy Dwarf craftsmanship won over. Caledor's sword shattered against Gotrek's hammer as a flawed Elf blade beaten upon a time-worn Dwarf anvil. Caledor cried for mercy, but the fires of retribution burned in the High King's eye, for he knew that the affront of the Elves would never be cowed with leniency. His hammer ended it, and Caledor, second Phoenix King of that name, was no more. In recompense the ~High King took the dead Elf's crown, and here in Karaz-a-Karak it remains to this day. Thus was the grip of the Elf claw on our lands broken, and they fled to their home shores weeping for their fallen. We showed them what real Dwarf mettle was like, and the War of Vengeance was our great victory. And yet, never have they apologised for their insults, and still yet there are unnumbered entries in the Great Book of Grudges that must be atoned for.

Never again, though, will Elf-kin make the mistake of rousing the ire of the sons of Grungni. Mark my words, that's how it was."

THE DWARF TONGUE

The ancient high language of the Dwarfs is called Khazalid. It is a deeply conservative language that has not changed noticeably in many thousands of years either in its spoken or written 'runic' form. The Dwarfs are very proud of their tongue which they rarely speak in the company of other races and never teach to other creatures. To humans it is the 'secret tongue of the Dwarfs', occasionally overheard, but never properly understood.

The Dwarf language includes very few words of obviously human or elvish origin. By contrast there are many loan words from Khazalid in the tongue of Men. This is most obviously so in the case of words to do with the traditional Dwarvish craftskills of masonry and smithying, skills which Men learned from the Dwarfs many centuries past. These loans from Khazalid mean that some Dwarf words sound very similar to equivalent human words.

Of course, some Khazalid words are all too familiar to the Dwarfs' enemies – namely the fearsome battlecries, oaths, and curses of the Dwarfs at war. Of these the most famous is the cry of '*Khazukan Kazakit-ha*' or its common shortened form of, '*Khazuk! Khazuk! Khazuk!*' which means 'Look out! The Dwarfs are on the warpath'. It is also usual for Dwarfs to call upon their ancestor gods during battle. It is said that the guttural sound of Dwarfs bellowing Grungni's name is enough to make an Elf's knees knock and a Goblin turn a sickly shade of yellow!

The sound of Khazalid is not much like human speech and very unlike the melodious sound of Elvish. Comparisons have been drawn to the rumble of thunder. All Dwarfs have very deep, resonant voices and a tendency to speak more loudly than is strictly necessary. This can make Dwarfs sound rowdy and irascible – which for the most part is a fair reflection of Dwarvish temperament. Khazalid vowel sounds in particular are uncompromisingly precise and heavily accented. Consonants are often spat aggressively or gargled at the back of the throat as if attempting to dislodge a recalcitrant gobbet of phlegm. A drinking hall full of loud, drunken Dwarfs sounds like a frightening place even when fists aren't flying – which isn't often.

The vocabulary of Khazalid ably reflects the unique pre-occupations of the Dwarf race. There are hundreds of words for different kinds of rock, for passages and tunnels, and most of all for precious metals. Indeed, there are hundreds of words for gold alone, reflecting on its qualities of colour, lustre, purity and hardness. When Dwarfs gather for an evening's drinking, which is most evenings, a popular entertainment is the Gold Song. During the Gold Song the Dwarfs sing about gold and each drinker sings a verse in turn. Each Dwarf must use a different word for gold when he sings his verse, and any Dwarf who repeats a word already sung or who is unable to think of another word for gold pays a forfeit. As the forfeit is inevitably to buy another round of drinks a Dwarf will often invent a new word for gold rather than admit defeat. If this new word goes unchallenged then he avoids the forfeit and another word for gold is invented.

In their dealings with others Dwarfs choose their words carefully. A Dwarf will not venture an opinion on anything that he has not considered deeply, and once his mind is made up you can be sure his view will be as immovable as a mountain. Dwarfs don't change their opinions except in the face of overwhelming necessity – and not always then. Many would rather die stubbornly than admit to a mistake that costs them their life! For this reason Dwarfs take oaths and promises very seriously indeed, and this extends to their business affairs even those with other races. In all the Dwarf language the word *Unbaraki* is the most condemning of all – it means 'oathbreaker'.

Given how seriously Dwarfs treat words their sense of humour tends to be especially unnerving. A common jest takes the form whereby two or more Dwarfs conspire to make another feel deeply uncomfortable by pretending to know something about his circumstances, state of health, or past life that in reality they do not. This can go on for hours, days, or many years and is generally reckoned to be very funny indeed. More commonly a Dwarf might make some provocative statement, wait for another to take offence, and then start a fight. Surprisingly these things tend to end in good humour, much back slapping and mutual congratulations with honour considered to have been satisfied all round.

THE RUNIC SCRIPT

Dwarf runes were invented for carving Khazalid onto stone, hence the letters are formed from straight lines which can be easily cut with a chisel. The script consists of a core alphabetic script which can be used to express any words, and additional individual runes each of which is a shorthand sign that represents a single word, idea, or name. This means that many words can be written in two forms – though this is only commonly seen with the names of people and places. Magical runes always take this second individual form and for this reason all non-alphabetic runes are regarded as having special significance or power.

Runes are usually carved left to right, but can also be carved in alternate rows starting from left to right, the second row right to left, the third left to right and so on. Runes can also be carved vertically from top to bottom, this being a common form for monuments and important carvings. Written forms generally go left to right horizontally.

The core alphabetic runes are called *Klinkarhun* which means 'chisel runes' and these are the most commonly used and easily recognised. Although the sound of Khazalid does not exactly match the sounds of human speech, the chart shown on the next page gives the closest approximations. The sounds should be pronounced with force and the 'r' and 'kh' sound in particular are made as if enthusiastically clearing the throat, whilst 'z' is always given extra emphasis as in 'buzz'.

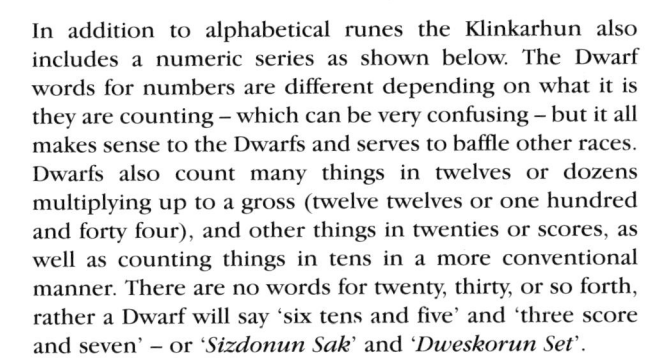

In addition to alphabetical runes the Klinkarhun also includes a numeric series as shown below. The Dwarf words for numbers are different depending on what it is they are counting – which can be very confusing – but it all makes sense to the Dwarfs and serves to baffle other races. Dwarfs also count many things in twelves or dozens multiplying up to a gross (twelve twelves or one hundred and forty four), and other things in twenties or scores, as well as counting things in tens in a more conventional manner. There are no words for twenty, thirty, or so forth, rather a Dwarf will say 'six tens and five' and 'three score and seven' – or '*Sizdonun Sak*' and '*Dweskorun Set*'.

KHAZALID – BASIC STRUCTURE

Whilst Khazalid undoubtedly has a formal grammatical structure it is very hard for an outsider to figure out what it might be. In general Khazalid places the subject before the verb and the object afterwards, but emphasis of pronunciation alone can sometimes determine a word's position within the structure of a sentence. In other cases the importance of a particular word can demand that it be placed first in the sentence. Such words are often placed first out of respect and then again in their proper place later on, for example, 'the King – I went to see the King.' When repeated words are written or carved they commonly appear as individual runes at the start of a sentence and Klinkarhun elsewhere.

The first principle of the Dwarf tongue is that almost all of its words represent solid physical things. There are surprisingly few specific words for abstract concepts. As a result many words double up as both a physical thing and an abstract concept strongly associated with that thing. For example, the root word for 'big-stone' is *kar* and the most common word for a mountain is *karaz* – the '*az*' ending denoting a single material thing or specific place. The same root word, *kar*, is also used to mean enduring in the form '*karak*' – the '*ak*' ending denoting an abstract concept. Thus Karaz-a-Karak, the name of the Dwarf capital, means 'enduring mountain' or literally 'big stony stone place', though the name is more attractively rendered into human speech as Everpeak.

Curiously the Dwarf word for the race of men is *umgi* whilst its abstract form of *umgak* means 'shoddy' – the Dwarf word being equivalent to 'man-made'. This demonstrates just how important it is to look at the end of Dwarf words – for it is these special 'signifiers' which usually tell you what the word actually means. There are many types of signifiers, some of which are given below, and by combining the different signifiers with root words it is possible to expand the basic Khazalid lexicon given in this book.

Although root words are often used on their own, many Khazalid words consist of a root word followed by one or more signifiers. So for example:

Root word	*Signifier (1)*	*Signifier (2)*
Kar-	-az	-i
Big stone	place	race, person, trade

Karazi = Mountain tribe/tribesman/mountaineer

Some root words don't exist in a separate form at all. If a root word consists entirely of consonants it is usually written with an extra 'a' at the end but this is dropped when a signifier is added. For example, 'Ska-' is the root for 'thief', 'theft' and 'to steal'.

Ska - az	Skaz = thief in general – 'a thief'
Ska - azi	Skazi = a specific thief – 'the thief'
Ska - ak	Skak = theft
Ska - it	Skit = steal

THE KLINKARHUN

A or I		Kar		1	Ong	9	Nuk
Ak		L or Ul		2	Tuk	10	Don
Az		M		3	Dwe	12	Duz
B		N		4	Fut	20	Skor
D		Ng		5	Sak	100	Kantuz
Dr or Tr		O		6	Siz	144	Groz (also means 'big' in a general sense)
E		R		7	Set		
F or V		T		8	Odro	1000	Milluz
G		Th					
H		W or U					
K or Kh		Z or Zh					

As in the example above – verb signifiers usually appear at the end of words. In Khazalid almost every noun has a verb form which is usually denoted by '-it'. In the present tense and 'ed' in the past. Tenses other than the simple present and past are denoted by additional words before the verb rather than by different endings – the equivalent to 'will steal' (*an skit*) in the simple future tense. Although separate words these are often written together as shown.

Skit	steal
Sked	stole
Anskit	will steal
Adsked	had stolen
Anadsked	will have stole

COMMON SIGNIFIERS

In the case of all signifiers a 'g' or 'k' can be added immediately before the signifier if the preceding root or signifier is a vowel or weak consonant such as 'l' or 'r'. This avoids placing two vowels together – which is something Dwarfish strenuously avoids. However there are no rules for this, and in many cases one of the vowels is simply missed out especially if it is the weaker vowel 'a' or 'i' (which are almost the same sound in Khazalid and the same rune in klinkarhun).

-az This is a very important and common signifier and it means the word represents a specific physical thing or place – a particular mountain not mountains in general. It is usually placed directly after the root before any other signifiers. That much is easy – unfortunately there are many things that the Dwarfs regard as so real and solid that the -az signifier is used even though they are talking about something which is neither a place or a material object! For example '*Galaz*' which means 'fearless'. In this case the -az refers to the 'real essence' of the idea. So, from the root '*Dur*' which means 'stone that can be riven' comes *Duraz* which means a stone slab but also *Durak* which means 'hard like a stone slab'. Although it is perfectly right to describe a tough Dwarf as *Durak* (rock hard) it would also be correct to describe him as *Duraz* (literally stone).

-ak This is the other major common signifier and means that the word represents a concept, something abstract such as honour, courage or fortitude. Of course, Dwarfs being Dwarfs, really important abstract concepts are accorded the status of real things, so 'a grudge to be avenged' is *Dammaz*, not *Dammak*, but *Dammak* still stands for the general concept of outstanding grudges.

-ar This signifies something that continues indefinitely over time – usually an activity such as trade (*urbar*) but also an experience such as chronic pain (*urtar*) and natural forces such as the movement of the sun (*Zonstrollar* – sun-walk-ing).

-en This signifies something that is currently ongoing but not indefinite such as journeying (*strollen*), marching (*gotten*) or carrying a heavy burden (*hunken*).

-i The signifier 'i' shows that the word refers to an individual person, or a profession, or race. In general it is most easily thought of as representing the definite article 'the' or even 'that person just there'. Many personal names end with this signifier too.

-al The signifier 'al' shows that the words refers to a group or band of people or creatures – rather like a collective noun. So, whilst the word for both the race of men and 'the man' is *umgi* a band of men is *umgal*. It is also used to encompass a person's kinsfolk in the form *Grummal* – Grumm's people often translated as Grummlings.

-it or -git This signifier when applied to a noun indicates something small or trivial. It is also used for a present tense verb – but Dwarfs are used to such things and rarely let it confuse them.

-ul or -kul This is a common word ending for Dwarf words and not always a signifier but often means 'the art of, understanding of, or master of', for example *Grungkul* the art of mining, and *Kazakul* the art of battle or generalship.

-ha This signifier always appears at the end of a word and is the equivalent to an exclamation mark. It is pronounced very abruptly and can be read as 'so there' or 'so watch it' – definitely fighting talk.

USEFUL ELEMENTS

The following useful words are the Dwarf equivalent of conjunctions, relative pronouns, and other common grammatical elements. Although words in their own right they are often appended directly before other words to form new compound words such as '*Okrik*' which means usurper King (literally Why-King) and *Aguz* which means 'replete' (literally with-food).

A	Of, with, within, to
Ad	Did, done, (preceding a verb)
Af	They, you (plural)
Ai, I, Ap and **Ip**	All forms of yes
An	Will/shall/am going to/with purpose (preceding a verb)
Anad	Will have done or shall have done
Bin	In, on, beside
Anu	Soon, very soon, any minute now!
Bar	But, bear in mind, except for (also the word for a fortified gate)
Ek	He, she, it, you (singular)
Nai, Na or **Nuf**	All forms of no, not, and never
Nu	Now, at this time
Ok	Why, how
Or	I, me, myself
Sar	May, could, might (preceding a verb)
Um	Them, those, these
Un	And
Ut	Us, we, ourselves
Wanrag	Where
Wanrak	When (preceding a verb),

Agrul	Stone carving; lines in face of very old Dwarf
Angaz	Ironwork
Ankor	Domain or realm
Arm	The Khazalid irregular verb to be (present tense arm – past tense urz)
Az	War axe
Azgal	Treasure hoard
Azul	Metal of any kind; dependable; a sturdy Dwarf
Bar	A fortified gateway or door
Barag	War machine
Baraz	A bond or promise
Boga	A candle which blows out unexpectedly plunging the tunnel into darkness
Bok	Banging your head on the roof of a low tunnel; characteristic scar on forehead caused by same!
Boki	Slang word for Dwarf miners
Bolg	Large fat belly. Also a state of extreme wealth, age and contentment
Bran	Clever, alert, mentally sharp
Bryn	Gold which shines strikingly in the sunlight; anything shiny or brilliant
Chuf	Piece of very old cheese a Dwarf miner keeps under his hat for emergencies
Dal	Old, good
Dammaz	A grievance, grudge, or insult to be avenged
Dammaz Kron	The Book of Grudges
Dar	A challenge or bet
Dawr	As good as something can get without it being proven over time and hard use. Most Dwarf words for 'good' imply age and reliability too but Dawr simply means 'looks like it might be good'. It literally translates as 'like Dwarf'.
Deb	New, untried, raw
Doh	Stupid, slow-witted, gullable
Dok	Watch, observe, see, the eye
Dongliz	The parts of a Dwarf's body impossible for him to scratch
Drakk	Dragon
Drek	Far, a great distance; great ambition or enterprise
Dreng	Slay in combat
Drengi	Slayer, one of the cult of Slayers
Drongnel	Dragon stew with cave mushrooms marinated in strong ale
Drung	To defeat, vanquish
Duk	Low, narrow tunnel
Dum	Doom or darkness
Durak	Hard
Duraz	Stone or slab
Dawi	Dwarfs
Ekrund	A stairway descending beneath the ground
Elgi	Elves
Elgram	Weak, enfeebled, thin
Elgraz	Construction that looks as if it is about to collapse
Endrinkuli	An engineer or mechanic (generally a Dwarf Engineer)
Frongol	Mushrooms which grow at the back of a cave
Galaz	Gold of particular ornamental value
Gand	Find, discover
Garaz	Fearless, rebellious
Gazan	Plains, wasteland
Gibal	Fragments of food enmeshed in a Dwarf's beard
Ginit	Small stone which works its way into your boot causing discomfort
Girt	Broad tunnel with plenty of headroom
Git	The Khazalid irregular verb to go (present tense git – past tense ged) the word is related to Got (ibid)
Gnol	Old, reliable, proven, wise
Gnoll-engrom	Respect due to a Dwarf who has a longer and more spectacular beard
Gor	Wild beast
Gorak	Great cunning, uncanny
Gorl	Gold which is especially soft and yellow; the colour yellow
Gorog	Ale; high spirits; a drinking binge
Got	March or travel quickly and with purpose
Grik	Pain in the neck caused by continually stooping in low tunnels
Grim	Harsh, unyielding
Grimaz	Barren place
Grindal	Long flaxen plaits worn by Dwarf maidens
Grint	Waste rock or spoil left by miners' excavations
Grizal	Poor meat
Grizdal	Ale which has been fermented for at least a century
Grob	The colour green, also Goblins and Orcs – literally greenies
Grobi	Goblins
Grobkaz	Goblin work, evil deeds
Grobkul	Art of stalking Goblins in caves
Grog	Inferior or watered ale; mannish brew
Grom	Brave or defiant
Gromdal	An ancient artefact
Gromthi	Ancestor
Grong	Anvil
Gronit	The Khazalid irregular verb to do (present tense gronit – past tense gird)
Gronti	Giant
Grumbak	A short measure of ale; trivial complaint or grumble
Grumbaki	A grumbler or whiner
Grund	Hammer
Grung	A mine
Grungnaz	Making or smithying
Grungni	Dwarf ancestor, god of mines and smiths
Grungron	A forge
Guz	To consume food or drink
Hazkal	Ale brewed recently; a fiery young warrior.
Hunk	Carry heavy rocks or other burden
Ik	Putting your hand in something slimy and unpleasant in the darkness
Irkul	Pillared vault hewn in rock
Kadrin	Mountain pass
Karag	Volcano or barren mountain
Karak	Enduring
Karaz	Mountain
Kazad	Fortress
Kazak	War or battle
Khaz	An underground hall
Khazukan	Dwarfs – literally hall-dwellers
Khrum	War drum
Klad	Armour
Klinka	Chisel
Klinkarhun	Common runes
Kol	Black stone, the colour black, sombre
Konk	Gold which is ruddy in colour; large and bulbous nose.
Krink	Bad back due to continual stooping
Kron	Book, record or history
Kruk	A seemingly promising vein of ore which gives out suddenly; an unexpected disappointment; a venture which comes to nothing
Krunk	Underground rockfall; a disaster!
Krut	A discomforting disease contracted from mountain goats
Kruti	A Dwarf suffering from Krut; a goatherd; an insult
Kulgur	The art of cooking Troll
Kuri	Meat stew boiled up by travelling Dwarfs from whatever ingredients are at hand. Traditionally spiced with wild berries
Lok	Highly embellished or intricate; praiseworthy
Makaz	Weapon or tool
Mingol	Tall watchtower built on lowland
Naggrund	An area of great upheaval, devastation, or industry
Nogarung	Drinking tankard made from a Troll's skull
Ogri	Ogre
Ok	Cunning or skilful
Okri	Craftsman - a common personal name
Onk	Comradely accretion of dirt and grime on company of Dwarfs who have spent many days underground
Ragarin	Coarse and uncomfortable clothing made from a Troll's hide
Rhun	Rune, word, or power
Rhunki	Runesmith
Rik	King or lord
Rikkit	A small stone which falls on your head as you walk down a tunnel
Ril	Gold ore which shines brightly in rock
Rinn	A Lady Dwarf; king's consort.
Rorkaz	Informal shouting contest
Ruf	A large underground dome either natural or constructed
Runk	A one-sided fight; a sound thrashing!
Rutz	Slackness of bowels caused by drinking too much ale
Skarrenruf	The colour bright blue, the day time sky
Skaz	Thief
Skof	A cold meal eaten underground
Skrat	To search for gold amongst rock debris or stream bed; scavenge; sparse living
Skrati	Poor prospector
Skree	Loose rock on mountain-side
Skruff	A scrawny beard; an outrageous insult!
Skrund	To hew rock; to get stuck in!
Skuf	A drunken brawl or skirmish
Slotch	The sodden mix of water, mud and pulverised stone found at the bottom of a mineworking
Stok	To hit or strike
Strol	Walk or travel leisurely
Stromez	Stream
Thag	Slay by act of treachery
Thagi	Murderous traitor
Thindrongol	Secret vault in which ale or treasure is hidden
Thingaz	Dense forest
Throng	Army; huge assembly of Dwarfs; a clan
Thrund	A hand gun
Trogg	A feast or heavy drinking bout
Troll	Troll
Tromm	Beard; respect due to age or experience.
Ufdi	A Dwarf overfond of preening and decorating his beard; a vain Dwarf; a Dwarf who cannot be trusted to fight.
Umanar	Roughly or approximately, and also indecision or vacillation
Umgak	Shoddy, poorly made
Umgi	Men
Unbaraki	An oathbreaker – there is nothing worse in Dwarf estimation.
Und	A watchpost carved into the mountain-side
Ungdrin Ankor	Underway, the ancient underground roadway of the Dwarfs.
Ungor	Cavern
Ungrim	A Dwarf who has not yet fulfilled an important oath; an untrustworthy Dwarf
Urbar	Trade
Urbaz	A trading post or market
Urk	Orc or enemy
Uzkul	Bones or death
Valdahaz	Brewery
Varn	Mountain lake
Vongal	Raiding band
Vorn	A farm
Wan	On its own at the start of a phrase Wan shows the phrase is a question. It's the Dwarf equivalent of a question mark. This is usually missed off where a standard Wan – question word is used instead (Wanrag, Wanrak, Wanrum). Wan – is also used immediately before another word to frame a question (Ek Wangit? 'are you going' literally 'you go?', Wandar 'is it good?' literally 'good?')
Wanaz	A disreputable Dwarf with an unkempt beard; an insult
Wattock	An unsuccessful Dwarf prospector; a down-at-heel Dwarf; an insult
Wazzok	A Dwarf who has exchanged gold or some other valuable item for something of little or no worth; a foolish or gullable Dwarf; an insult
Werit	A Dwarf who has forgotten where he placed his tankard of ale; a state of befuddlement
Wutroth	Wood from ancient mountain oak
Zak	An isolated hut in the mountains
Zaki	A crazed Dwarf who wanders in the mountains
Zan	Blood, the colour red
Zharr	Fire
Zhuf	Waterfall or rapidly flowing river
Zorn	Upland plateau or high meadow
Zon	Sun

DWARF TACTICS

LEADING YOUR DWARFS

Gav Thorpe

Dwarfs are everything you could want from infantry regiments. They are sturdy, brave and skilled in close combat. They can have considerable missile fire and devastating war engines to back up their infantry units. However, there is also one obvious downside to using Dwarfs – they won't be winning any races! Below are some suggestions for plans that get the most out of your army's strengths and minimise its drawbacks.

THE ENDURING MOUNTAIN

The Dwarf army's lack of mobile units such as cavalry and chariots is seen by many players as a disadvantage, but this is not so! With none of these units to cloud your thinking, you can devise a proper Dwarfish plan of action. The obvious strategy is to assume a defensive position and then watch the enemy dash themselves onto your rock hard units. A clever opponent will try to avoid your toughest units and snatch Victory points from 'softer' targets such as war engines and missile troops. Any defensive plan must take this into account and attempt to protect these more vulnerable units.

The best defensive deployment is around a hill as shown in diagrams A and B, as this allows you to place war engines and missile troops behind a force of dedicated close combat units. Your first line should consist of solid units of Warriors, Longbeards, Hammerers and/or Ironbreakers. Place your General and a Battle Standard (best with the Master Rune of Stromni Redbeard) near the centre and it will have to be an exceedingly strong or lucky enemy to break through head-on. However, a canny enemy will not try to smash through your lines by direct assault unless he has no other choice, instead he will attempt to move around the ends of your line, (known as the flanks).

Always endeavour to discourage the enemy from trying to outflank you in this manner with your Troll Slayers, Organ Guns or Flame Cannons. The unbreakable Troll Slayers are a great obstacle for any opposing unit trying to make a quick breakthrough to your more vulnerable missile and war engine units. As the Slayers do not have to worry too much about combat resolution, you can deploy them in a fairly wide but shallow formation which is difficult for the enemy to get around. Flame Cannons and Organ Guns, on the other hand, are not particularly strong in close combat but can devastate enemy units that manoeuvre to charge them. Often your opponent will be unwilling to take them on with his best troops, which is good for you as it means that these regiments will be in the centre of his line, facing off against your hardest units.

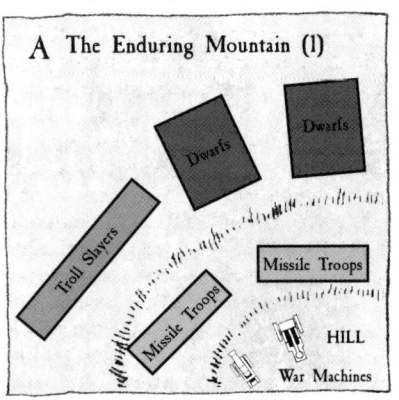

Behind this rampart of solid Dwarf warriors, your Crossbows, Thunderers and war engines can pound upon the enemy, keeping up a constant bombardment from the very first turn. Except against an opponent wholly dedicated to shooting back at you (as you may find with Elves, for example) this punishment will force the enemy to come forward to deal with your ranged attacks, and that's just what you want them to do. When they arrive, the enemy will be weakened by your fusillade and be no match for your strong regiments of proud Dwarfs.

THE BEAR TRAP

The Enduring Mountain is good if there is a position for your war engines and missile troops to occupy behind your protecting regiments. If there is no such feature, the Bear Trap can be used instead. Put simply, this plan puts your missile troops and war engines in the centre of the line, with your harder units to either flank. If the enemy moves to attack the units in the centre, the wings (the teeth of the trap) can move in on their flanks, trapping and destroying opposing units. If the enemy refuses the bait, which is likely, you have once again managed to ensure that your enemies confront your close combat units.

With the Bear Trap it is important not to spread your army too thinly and to ensure that the flanks of the line are secure. Isolated Dwarf units are easier for the enemy to destroy, as they can be more readily charged in the flank which negates their rank bonus and also increases your opponent's combat resolution score. When deploying their army, many players automatically line up along the length of the table, parallel to the enemy army. This doesn't have to be the case, and if you set up your Bear Trap at a slight angle, this means that the edges of the battlefield are protecting your flanks. See diagram C to see how this works.

A The Enduring Mountain (1)

B The Enduring Mountain (2)

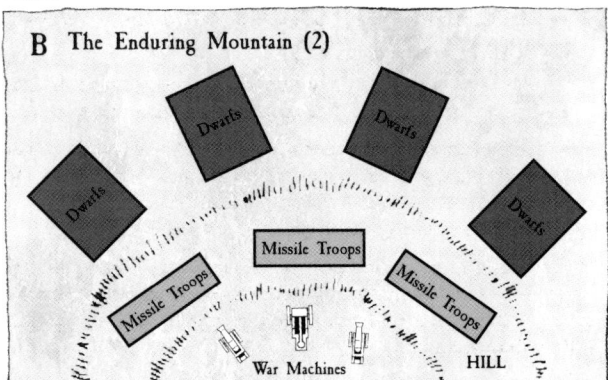

C The Bear Trap (1)

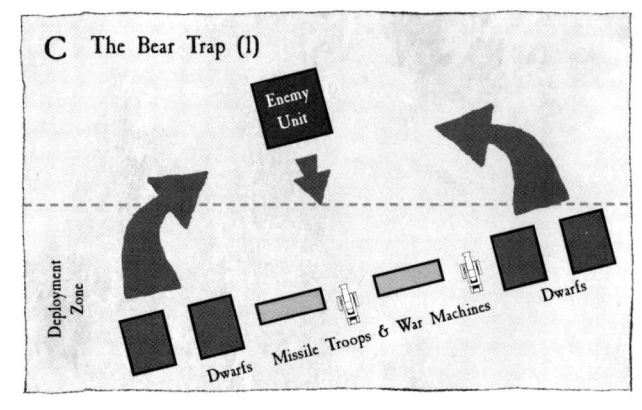

D The Bear Trap (2)

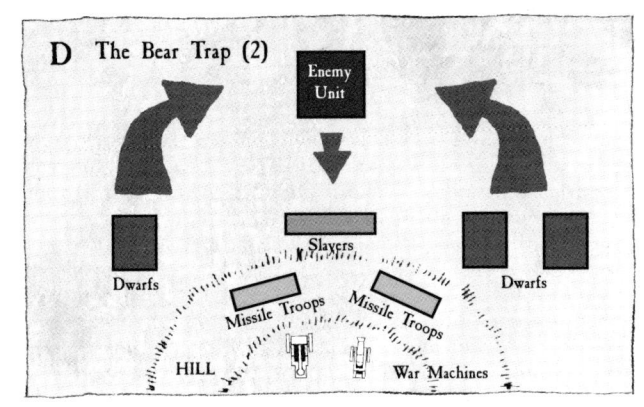

[Diagram showing Enemy Unit at top, with curved arrows flanking around to meet Dwarf units on either side, Slayers in centre front, Missile Troops behind, and War Machines with Hill at the back.]

The Bear Trap can actually be combined with the Enduring Mountain as a variation, as shown in diagram D above.

THE HAMMER

One way to catch the enemy off guard is to attack! Not many players are prepared for a Dwarf army marching towards them, and it can throw their own plans off. Against an enemy with anything remotely fast (like cavalry, flyers or chariots) the Hammer plan works best if only close combat units and perhaps a Gyrocopter or two are taken. This is because your units are going to steamroller towards the enemy, and missile or war engine units will get left behind and be vulnerable to enemies sweeping around your flanks.

When using the Hammer, deploy slightly to one side of the centre of the tabletop so that one flank of the advancing army is against the table edge and therefore safe from being outflanked. As with the Enduring Mountain, the other flank can be protected with Gyrocopters and Slayers. The Hammer is a brutally simple strategy – the aim is to get your hardest units into combat with the hardest enemy units. Once there, the sturdiness of your warriors can usually grind down all but the most intimidating opposition.

MINERS, RANGERS AND GYROCOPTERS

All three of the plans outlined above are really geared towards achieving one aim — to get the enemy fighting your toughest units rather than more vulnerable missile regiments and artillery. Miners, Rangers and Gyrocopters can all prove invaluable in this.

Miners can be used in two ways. The first is to take them out of your figure case and leave them on a side table, so that your opponent knows that they're under the ground somewhere, just waiting to turn up on his flank or behind

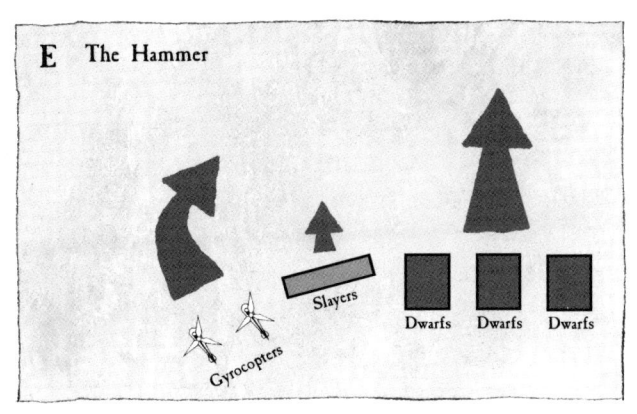

E The Hammer

[Diagram showing Gyrocopters on left flank with curved arrow, Slayers centre, three Dwarfs units on right advancing forward with large arrow.]

his army. This may make your enemy more cautious, perhaps not straying too close to the table edges, or leaving units behind to guard vulnerable war machines, that sort of thing. The second is to spring them as a surprise if you can. Imagine a Skaven or Orc player streaming towards your rows of cannons and crossbows as fast as possible – only to find that a 20 strong unit, ranked up and armed with Great weapons, appears on his flank, stopping some of his units from marching and ready to charge next turn. Being able to force your opponent to alter his plans, taking some of the initiative and impetus from him, is a valuable asset.

Rangers can be used similarly, but must be deployed carefully. It's better to put them in your deployment zone and ignore their Scouts ability than to set them up in a poor position just because you can. The same goes for Miners sometimes – against certain opposing set-ups or very fast enemy (such as Bretonnians) you may like to deploy them just like any other close combat unit rather than risk having to wait around for them to turn up.

Rangers can be used in two ways as well, depending on whether you want to mainly defend or attack. Used defensively, they act as a roadblock, slowing the enemy and gaining more time for your Stone Throwers and Thunderers to rain death upon them from afar. Eventually your Rangers will get broken or wiped out, but as long as they sell their lives as dearly as possible, their effort will be worth it. Used aggressively, Rangers should press forward towards the enemy, perhaps going after enemy skirmishers and Scouts (they probably won't get them, but it'll stop them being a nuisance to your army), or moving along a flank to threaten war engines and the like. Try not to leave them on their own for too long though – get the rest of your army heading towards the enemy from the start.

If there's one thing bound to spoil a Dwarf lord's day it's marauding fast cavalry, flyers and skirmishers. These can cause no end of havoc, charging your units in the flanks, loitering in a threatening manner near your war engines and so on. This is where a Gyrocopter comes in handy. Able to dash about the battlefield, Gyrocopters can counter these kinds of threats. Such units are generally lightly armoured and so make perfect targets for the steam cannon. These flying war engines can also be used to stop the enemy from marching, which gives you two options. Firstly, an enemy forced to move at normal speed towards a defensive force will suffer more casualties from missile fire. Alternatively, those fast flanking Wolf Riders, Elyrian Reavers and the like can be slowed down with a well placed Gyrocopter, allowing you more time to react with other units. With either of these tactics, remember to leave the Gyrocopter in a position where it cannot be charged – if the enemy get into combat it'll more than likely be forced to crash.

With the little room that's left, here's a few quick things to consider:

Pick a plan and stick to it when choosing your army, and remember to take runes that complement this strategy.

Don't underestimate the usefulness of Bolt Throwers. When the armies start getting mixed in with each other, they can pick off monsters and the like without risking a stone or cannon ball smashing through your own units.

Dwarf war engine crews are more sturdy than Orcs, Men or Elves, so against light enemy troops (such as Scouts or fast cavalry) it is sometimes worthwhile standing and fighting rather than fleeing.

And finally, never trust an Elf!

ARMIES OF THE DWARFS

What follows is a selection of alternative army lists you can use when playing with a Dwarf force. These lists alter the selection of different units available, and may not be as balanced as the main army list. For this reason you should agree with your opponent beforehand that you'll be picking one of the armies given here. You may like to write a special scenario for your variant army to take part in, or maybe your force has a part to play in an ongoing campaign.

GUILD EXPEDITION

The Engineers Guild is separate from the clans of a Hold and is able to muster an army of its own. Often this force is used for forays across the mountains to other Holds, or to accompany trade convoys to the towns of Men, guarding valuable Dwarf inventions and artefacts, or the gold paid for them. As you might expect, the Guild has access to many war engines and blackpowder weapons, and a Guild Expedition relies heavily upon this massed firepower. One of the greatest Guild expeditions took place three hundred years ago when Guildmaster 'Wondergun' Thorkesson took fifteen wagons of weapons to Marienburg, all the way across the Empire. They fought jealous Imperial lords, roving bandits, Beastmen warbands and marauding Orcs and Goblins. They lost only one wagon – it was carrying handgun ammunition which they were forced to expend along the way.

CHARACTERS

No Slayer characters may be taken. All Thanes (Master Engineers) and Dwarf Lords (Guild Masters) have the Artillery Master and Extra Crewman rules, costing +35 points for a Thane and +45 points for a Lord. A Runelord or Runesmith cannot be your General.

CORE UNITS

Warriors, Thunderers, Cannons, Stone Throwers, Bolt Throwers (up to two per choice).

You must have a unit of Warriors for every two cannons, Stone Throwers, or Bolt Throwers (choices, not models) in your expedition.

SPECIAL UNITS

Gyrocopters, 0-2 Organ Guns, 0-2 Flame Cannons.

RARE UNITS

Rangers, Longbeards, Dogs of War.

THRONG OF KARAK KADRIN

Karak Kadrin is noted amongst the Holds for its Slayer King. In ages past, King Baragor swore the Slayer oath, reportedly for the terrible shame he felt when a Dragon slew his daughter as she travelled to Karaz-a-Karak to marry the High King. However, he could not renounce his vows as King, and although he wished to seek a glorious death in battle, he could not forswear his oath to protect and lead his people. Torn between these two conflicting duties, Baragor was driven to the edge of his sanity until finally his counsellors devised a solution which would satisfy his honour. Baragor founded the Shrine of Grimnir at Karak Kadrin, and donated many funds to the Slayer cult. To this day, Baragor's descendants have shared his twin vows, never able to unite the two completely, and they are considered slightly unhinged by Dwarfs of other Holds. Many Slayers make a pilgrimage to the Shrine of Grimnir and Karak Kadrin is known as the unofficial home of the Slayer cult, if such a thing could exist for these wanderers.

CHARACTERS

You may only take Slayer characters. One Daemon Slayer may be the Slayer King and has the same army list options as a Dwarf Lord. The Slayer King has a basic value of 220 points. One Slayer character must be your General, but this has no effect other than for Victory points purposes.

CORE UNITS

Slayers.

SPECIAL UNITS

Warriors, 0-1 Hammerers *(only if the Slayer King is present).*

RARE UNITS

Crossbowmen, Thunderers.

ROYAL CLAN

Each Dwarf Hold is home to many clans – the larger Karaks, such as Karaz-a-Karak, have over a hundred different ones living within their halls. The richest clans can obviously afford the best weapons and armour for their warriors, their extensive treasuries and armouries can be opened up in times of war so that they can field the most impressive and skilled warriors. Of all the clans, that of the Hold's King is invariably the richest, as he takes a tax of all the money made by the other clans. When the King's clan goes to war, he is able to draw on his large wealth to equip the best warriors of the Hold with the finest wargear, and in times of great need may even hire in mercenaries to defend the Hold. Also, the King can assemble all of his bodyguard, the Hammerers. The greatest army in the Dwarf empire is that of the High King of Karaz-a-Karak, and it is said that the ground trembles when this mighty host marches to war.

CHARACTERS
Must be led by a Dwarf Lord. No Slayer characters.

CORE UNITS
Hammerers (all the units are *stubborn*), 0-1 Ironbreakers, 0-1 Longbeards, Warriors.

SPECIAL UNITS
Thunderers, Crossbowmen, 0-1 Miners, 0-1 Rangers.

RARE UNITS
Cannons, Bolt Throwers (up to two per choice), Stone Throwers, Dogs of War.

OVERGROUND DEFENCE

At times it is necessary for a Dwarf army to be mustered to hold off an enemy force that is attacking the Hold's lands. This defence force is gathered from the outposts and settlements surrounding the Hold to buy time for a suitable army to be raised within the Karak. From distant mines and watchtowers the army assembles, joined by Slayers who hear of the approaching battles. Gyrocopters buzz from hilltop to hilltop taking news of the mustering to the commander of the defence force, and to report back events in the field to the King.

CORE UNITS
Rangers, Crossbowmen, 0-2 Miners.

SPECIAL UNITS
Warriors, Thunderers, 0-1 Slayers.

RARE UNITS
Gyrocopters, Longbeards, Dogs of War.

> Revere the ancestors, obey your king, bear your arms with pride, fear no foe, hate the Greenskin, mistrust the Elf, and you can do no wrong.
> — Old Dwarf saying

UNDGRIN ANKOR FORCE

The Undgrin Ankor is the network of underground corridors and highways that once linked all of the Dwarf empire in the Worlds Edge mountains. Nowadays much of it is shattered, and broken into by Skaven and Goblin tunnels, and sizeable forces are used to patrol its depths. Such Underway forces are also mustered to make expeditions into fallen Holds, their expertise at underground fighting essential in the foe-infested depths of places such as Karak Azgal and Karak Drazh.

CORE UNITS
Miners, 0-3 Ironbreakers.

SPECIAL UNITS
Warriors, 0-2 Longbeards, Thunderers, 0-1 Slayers.

RARE UNITS
Organ Gun.

WAR OF VENGEANCE

During the War of Vengeance, the time the Elves call the War of the Beard, the whole of the Dwarf empire was mobilised to fight against the kin of Ulthuan. The bravest veterans took up their arms to do battle once more, and the whole Dwarf race was possessed by a great need for vengeance against the Elves who had betrayed them so callously. During the War of the Beard the Dwarf realm was yet mighty and had not been laid low by volcanoes and earthquakes, and the Orcs and Goblins had not overrun many of the Dwarf Holds. At this time, even the Dwarfs had not discovered the secrets of black powder weapons, relying instead upon more traditional war machines.

All units in the army *hate* Elves (any type) instead of greenskins. No model may have a Dwarf handgun or pistol.

CORE UNITS
Warriors, Crossbowmen, 0-2 Longbeards, 0-1 Slayers, 0-1 Miners.

SPECIAL UNITS
0-1 Rangers, 0-1 Hammerers, Iron Breakers, Stone Thrower, Bolt Thrower (up to two per choice).

RARE UNITS
None.

FORCES OF THE DWARFS

Lords	M	WS	BS	S	T	W	I	A	Ld	Special Rules
Lord	3	7	4	4	5	3	4	4	10	Ancestral Grudge; Resolute; Relentless
Runelord	3	6	4	4	5	3	3	2	10	Ancestral Grudge; Resolute; Relentless; +1 Dispel dice
Daemon Slayer	3	7	3	4	5	3	5	4	10	Ancestral Grudge; Resolute; Relentless; Slayer; Unbreakable; Loner

Heroes	M	WS	BS	S	T	W	I	A	Ld	Special Rules
Thane	3	6	4	4	4	2	3	3	9	Ancestral Grudge; Resolute; Relentless
Runesmith	3	5	4	4	4	2	2	2	9	Ancestral Grudge; Resolute; Relentless; +1 Dispel dice
Engineer	3	4	4	3	4	2	2	1	9	Ancestral Grudge; Resolute; Relentless; Artillery Master; Extra Crewman
Dragon Slayer	3	6	3	4	4	2	4	3	10	Ancestral Grudge; Resolute; Relentless; Slayer; Unbreakable; Loner

Core units	M	WS	BS	S	T	W	I	A	Ld	Special Rules
Warrior	3	4	3	3	4	1	2	1	9	Ancestral Grudge; Resolute; Relentless
Crossbowman	3	4	3	3	4	1	2	1	9	Ancestral Grudge; Resolute; Relentless
Thunderer	3	4	3	3	4	1	2	1	9	Ancestral Grudge; Resolute; Relentless
Miner	3	4	3	3	4	1	2	1	9	Ancestral Grudge; Resolute; Relentless; Underground Advance
Ranger	3	4	3	3	4	1	2	1	9	Ancestral Grudge; Resolute; Relentless; Scouts; Foresters

Special units	M	WS	BS	S	T	W	I	A	Ld	Special Rules
Hammerer	3	5	3	4	4	1	2	1	9	Ancestral Grudge; Resolute; Relentless; Bodyguard
Longbeard	3	5	3	4	4	1	2	1	9	Ancestral Grudge; Resolute; Relentless; Immune to Panic
Ironbreaker	3	5	3	4	4	1	2	1	9	Ancestral Grudge; Resolute; Relentless
Troll Slayer	3	4	3	3	4	1	2	1	10	Ancestral Grudge; Resolute; Relentless; Slayer; Unbreakable
Cannon	–	–	–	–	7	3	–	–	–	See pages 122-124 of the Warhammer Rulebook
Bolt Thrower	–	–	–	–	7	3	–	–	–	See pages 124-125 of the Warhammer Rulebook
Stone Thrower	–	–	–	–	7	3	–	–	–	See pages 120-121 of the Warhammer Rulebook
Artillery Crew	3	4	3	3	4	1	2	1	9	Ancestral Grudge; Resolute; Relentless

Rare units	M	WS	BS	S	T	W	I	A	Ld	Special Rules
Flame Cannon	–	–	–	–	7	3	–	–	–	See page 15
Organ Gun	–	–	–	–	7	3	–	–	–	See page 16
Gyrocopter	–	–	–	–	5	3	–	–	–	See page 17
Pilot	–	4	–	3	–	–	2	1	9	See page 17

Champions	M	WS	BS	S	T	W	I	A	Ld	Champion's unit
Veteran	3	4	3	3	4	1	2	2	9	Warriors; Crossbowmen; Thunderers; Rangers
Prospector	3	4	3	3	4	1	2	2	9	Miners
Gate Keeper	3	5	3	4	4	1	2	2	9	Hammerers
Greatbeard	3	5	3	4	4	1	2	2	9	Longbeards
Ironbeard	3	5	3	4	4	1	2	2	9	Ironbreakers
Giant Slayer	3	5	3	4	4	1	3	2	10	Slayers

DWARF ARMOURY

GROMRIL ARMOUR: 4+ armour save

DWARF HANDGUN

Maximum Range: 24"; **Strength:** 4

Rules: Armour piercing

Superior design: A handgun has a +1 to hit modifier when firing at short range.

ORGAN GUN

1) Align Organ Gun on target.
2) Roll the Artillery dice and measure range. If the target unit is within range (up to 18") it will suffer a number of hits equal to the number rolled on the Artillery dice.
3) If the Artillery dice is a MISFIRE refer to the Organ Gun Misfire chart.
4) Work out all hits at Strength 5 with a -3 Armour save.

DWARF CANNON

1) Align the Cannon on the target and guess range (up to 48").
2) Roll the Artillery dice and add the score to the distance aimed. The cannon ball travels forward this distance before striking the ground.
3) If you roll a MISFIRE refer to the Misfire chart. Otherwise, mark the point where the cannon ball strikes the ground and roll the Artillery dice to establish the bounce distance. All models in the path of the bounce are hit.
4) If you roll a MISFIRE for the Bounce roll, the cannon ball sticks in the ground and does not bounce.
5) Work out hits at Strength 10. Wounding hits cause D3 wounds. No armour saving throw is allowed.

GYROCOPTER STEAM GUN

1) Align the Gyrocopter on the target.
2) Place the Flame template with the broad end over the target and the narrow end touching the muzzle of the Gyrocopter's steam gun. Models which are completely under the Flame template are hit automatically and models only partially covered are hit on the roll of a 4+.
3) Work out all hits at Strength 3 with an armour save modifier of -1.

STONE THROWER

1) Declare target & guess range (up to 60").
2) Position the 3" template and roll Scatter and Artillery dice.
3) If the Artillery dice is a MISFIRE, refer to Misfire Chart, otherwise...
   a) If the Scatter dice is a HIT, the stone has struck home.
   b) If the Scatter dice is an arrow the stone has landed in the direction shown 2", 4", 6", 8" or 10" away from the aiming point as shown on the Artillery dice.
4) All models completely under the template are hit. Those partially under are hit on a 4+.
5) Work out hits at S4. Each wounding hit causes D6 wounds. (A model at the centre of the template suffers a S8 hit). No armour save is allowed.

FLAME CANNON

1) Align the Flame Cannon on target and declare the distance you are aiming, up to a maximum of 12".
2) Roll the Artillery dice and add the score to the distance aimed. The burst of flame spurts through the air and lands at this point.
3) If you roll a MISFIRE refer to the Flame Cannon Misfire chart.
4) Place the thin end of the Flame template where the flame lands and the larger end extending directly away from the Flame Cannon. All models completely under the template are hit, models not completely under the template are hit on the roll of a 4+.
5) Resolve the effects of all hits at Strength 5 and -2 armour save.
6) Any units taking casualties must take an immediate Panic test.